Cleats & Eats Seattle

a boater's restaurant guide to the waters of greater Seattle

Second Edition

By Lorena Landon

Printed and bound in United States of America.

Third Printing, Second Edition April 2006

Published by
Woodland Cove Press
9805 NE 116th Street, PMB 7346
Kirkland, WA 98034
425-894-6016 FAX 425-820-9255
woodlandcovepress@att.net

We encourage you to notify us of any additions or changes for this publication. This publication is available at bulk discounts for corporate gifts, conventions, and fund-raising events.

ISBN-10: 0-9741380-0-2

ISBN-13: 978-0-9741380-0-8

Table of Contents

Preface

Seattle is one of the most unique and beautiful cities in the United States. Encircled by mountains and bodies of fresh water and salt water, and possessing the second largest ferry system in the world, this city offers a variety of pleasurable outdoor activities. It is no wonder that those of us who have grown up in the Pacific Northwest have a special place in our hearts for Seattle and its environs.

Boating is definitely a life style in the "Emerald City" and those lucky enough to live on or near the water, know that a whole new world of discovery awaits them. One of the many pleasures of living on the waterways of Seattle is arriving at a restaurant by boat. There are many restaurants accessible by water, some of which are not especially visible at first glance. This guide helps boaters locate docks available to the public for purposes of dining, where to tie-up, and which restaurants are accessible from each dock or landing. After many years of boating on Lake Washington and the Seattle area, it became apparent that such a guide would be helpful to the boating community. It is a pleasure to provide this restaurant guide to the community for our fellow boaters.

I would like to thank my husband, Leonard, for developing the dock diagrams, drawings, and layout for this publication. Special thanks to our friend, Steve Greaves, for his characterization of "Mr. Cleat" and his continued support. Steve was instrumental in helping us produce the first edition of Cleats & Eats.

Lorena Landon

Navigating this Book

Information in this guide is organized by watercraft landing and shown with a cleat icon. Each landing location, or "Cleats" section, contains two pages of information with photos and diagrams about the landing and tie-up space. Each landing has an associated "Eats" section with information about the restaurants accessible from that landing. Because of the extensive list of restaurants accessible from Kirkland's Marina Park, Madison Park Landing, and the 24th Avenue Landing, the "Eats" section for these landings consists of tables listing restaurants and eateries accessible within ¼ mile of the respective landing, and are listed according to type. The "Cleats" and associated "Eats" information is grouped and ordered by body of water and then by area name.

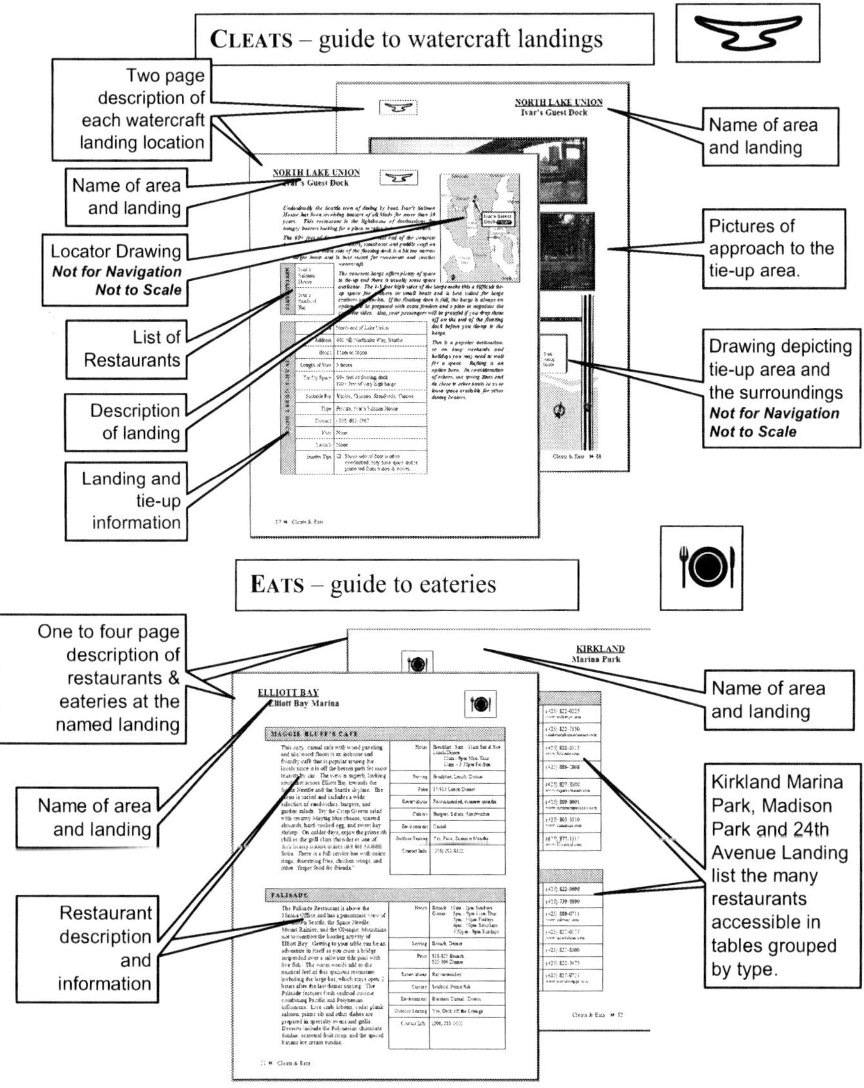

Reference Drawing

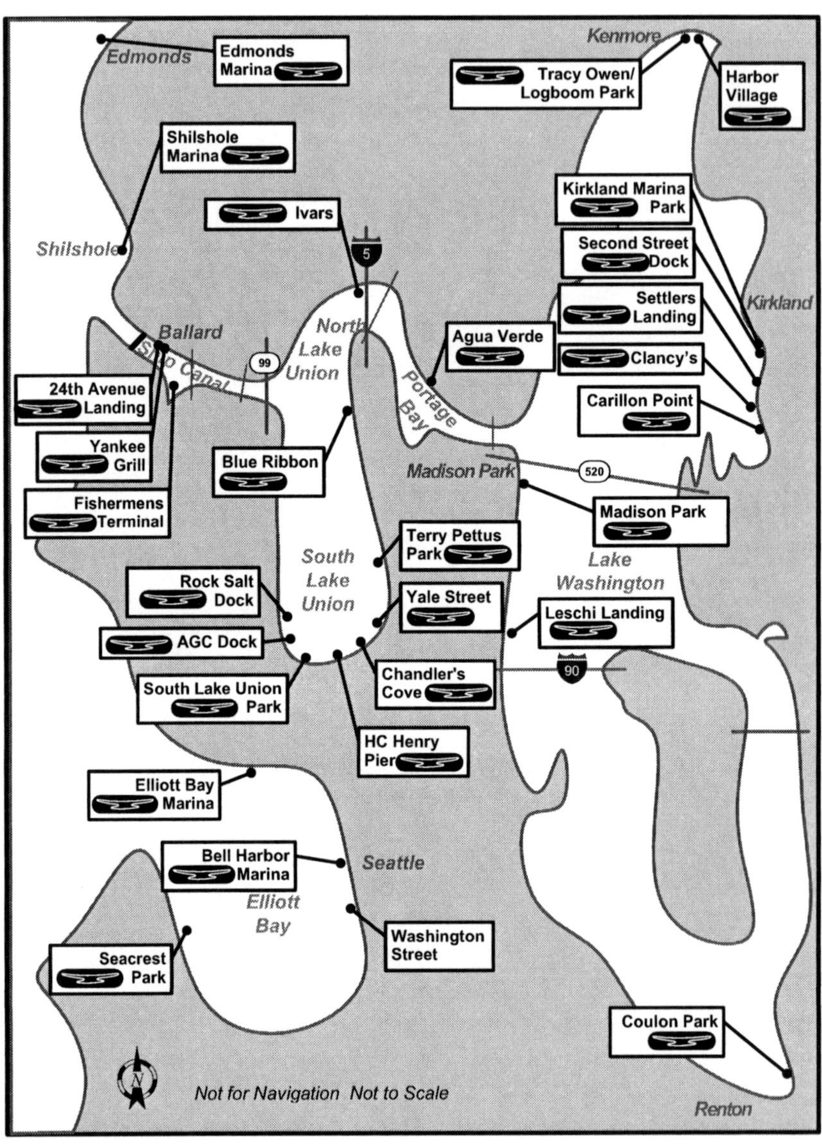
Edmonds
Edmonds Marina
Kenmore
Tracy Owen/ Logboom Park
Harbor Village
Shilshole Marina
Kirkland Marina Park
Ivars
Second Street Dock
Shilshole
Settlers Landing
Kirkland
North Lake Union
Agua Verde
Ballard
Clancy's
Ship Canal
99
Portage Bay
Carillon Point
24th Avenue Landing
Yankee Grill
Blue Ribbon
Madison Park
520
Fishermens Terminal
Madison Park
Terry Pettus Park
Lake Washington
South Lake Union
Rock Salt Dock
Yale Street
Leschi Landing
AGC Dock
Chandler's Cove
90
South Lake Union Park
HC Henry Pier
Elliott Bay Marina
Bell Harbor Marina
Seattle
Elliott Bay
Washington Street
Seacrest Park
Coulon Park
Not for Navigation Not to Scale
Renton

Index – by – Landing/Tie-up

Index – by – Landing/Tie-up

Index – by – Landing/Tie-up

EDMONDS, SHILSHOLE BAY & SHIP CANAL

Index – by – Restaurant

Index – by – Restaurant

Fuel Docks

Edmonds

Port of Edmonds (ask for Fuel Dock)	(425) 774-0549 (425) 775-4588

Elliott Bay

Elliott Bay Fuel Dock	(206) 282-8424

Lake Union

Morrison's North Star	(206) 284-6600

Lake Washington

Cap Sante, Kenmore	(425) 482-9465
Mercer Marine, Bellevue	(425) 641-2090
Yarrow Bay, Kirkland	(425) 822-6066

Shilshole Bay

Shilshole Bay Fuel Dock	(206) 783-7555

Ship Canal

Ballard Oil	(206) 783-0241
Covich-Williams	(206) 784-0171
Texaco Shilshole	(206) 783-7555

Index – by – Watercraft

	Page	Yachts	Cruisers	Runabouts	Canoes
Elliott Bay					
Bell Harbor Marina	13	X	X	X	
Elliott Bay Marina	19	X	X	X	
Seacrest Park	23	X	X	X	
Washington Street Park	27		Closed		
Lake Washington					
Kenmore, Harbor Village Marina	31	X	X	X	
Kenmore, Tracy Owen Park	35		X	X	X
Kirkland, Carillon Point Guest Dock	37	X	X	X	X
Kirkland, Clancy's Foghorn Dock	43	X	X	X	X
Kirkland, Marina Park	47	X	X	X	X
Kirkland, Second Street Dock	53	X	X	X	
Kirkland, Settlers Landing	57		X	X	
Leschi, Leschi Landing	61		X	X	X
Madison Park,Madison Park Landing	65	X	X		
Renton, Coulon Park	69	X	X	X	X
Portage Bay					
Agua Verde	75			X	X
North Lake Union					
Blue Ribbon Cooking	79		X	X	
Ivar's Guest Dock	83	X	X	X	X
Terry Pettus Park	87			X	X
South Lake Union					
AGC Building Guest Dock	93		X	X	
Chandler's Cove Guest Dock	97	X	X	X	X
H.C. Henry Pier	101	X	X	X	
Rock Salt Guest Dock	105	X	X	X	
South Lake Union Park	109			X	X
Yale Street Landing	113	X	X	X	
Edmonds					
Edmonds Marina	119	X	X	X	
Shilshole Bay					
Shilshole Bay Marina	123	X	X	X	
Ship Canal					
Fishermen's Terminal	129		X	X	
Yankee Grill Guest Dock	135	X	X	X	
24th Avenue Landing	139	X	X	X	

The groupings and tabular information in this index, and the "Suitable For" information in each landing or tie-up table, is intended to give the reader a general indication of the approximate size and type of watercraft suitable for each landing or tie-up space. It is not intended to refer to a specific type or length of watercraft. The reader and watercraft operator should make his or her own determination of the suitability of each landing or tie-up area for their own particular watercraft.

Elliott Bay

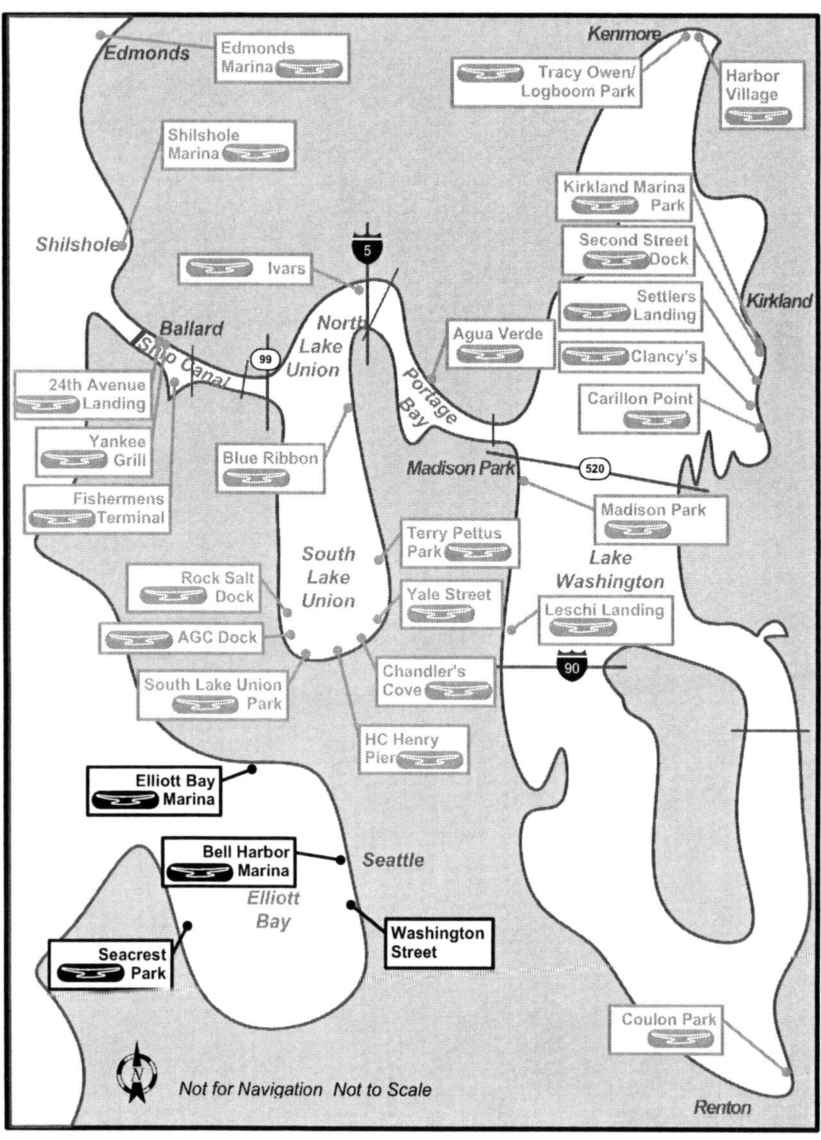

Edmonds
Edmonds Marina
Kenmore
Tracy Owen/ Logboom Park
Harbor Village
Shilshole Marina
Kirkland Marina Park
Shilshole
Second Street Dock
Ivars
5
Settlers Landing
Kirkland
North Lake Union
Ballard
Ship Canal
Agua Verde
99
Clancy's
24th Avenue Landing
Portage Bay
Carillon Point
Yankee Grill
Blue Ribbon
Madison Park
520
Fishermens Terminal
Madison Park
Terry Pettus Park
South Lake Union
Lake Washington
Rock Salt Dock
Yale Street
Leschi Landing
AGC Dock
90
Chandler's Cove
South Lake Union Park
HC Henry Pier
Elliott Bay Marina
Bell Harbor Marina
Seattle
Elliott Bay
Washington Street
Seacrest Park
Coulon Park
N
Not for Navigation Not to Scale
Renton

ELLIOTT BAY

Bell Harbor Marina

Visiting Seattle's waterfront and Seattle's public market by boat is a viable option thanks to the development of the Bell Harbor Marina located at Pier 66. The hourly transient moorage spaces are located along the main pier north of the A dock, between A and B docks, and between B and C docks, which are marked as "HOURLY." Hourly rates are $10 for 0-4 hours plus $5 for each additional hour regardless of length. Upon arrival, check in at the kiosk office to make payment and to receive a gate access code. If arriving after hours, payment should be made at the self-pay box on the office door. See the security guard for an access gate code.

Overnight stays are $1.25 per foot for boats 50 feet and under and $1.50 per foot for boats over 50 feet. Holiday rates are $1.75 per foot for all boats. The Marina can handle up to 120 foot vessels and offers showers, restrooms, and power. Call ahead for reservations and space assignment. Office hours are typically 7am-5pm winter months and 7am-7 pm during the summer months with a security guard on-site after hours.

Five restaurants and one coffee shop are all easily accessible from the Marina. The waterfront trolley stops on Alaskan Way across from the Marina, so if you have time and want to explore Seattle's beautiful waterfront with its many shops and restaurants, you can ride the trolley, which runs the length of the waterfront approximately every 20 minutes, seven days a week. You may get off at any of the numerous stops along the way.

To explore Seattle's famous Pike Place Market, look for the large set of stairs on the east side of Alaskan Way, which leads up to the market. Children will enjoy the Odyssey Maritime Discovery Center, located at the Bell Harbor landing; and the Seattle Aquarium located south of Bell Harbor on the waterfront.

RESTAURANTS
Anthony's
Anthony's Fish Bar
Bell Street Deli
Fish Club
Starbucks
Trolley Cafe

BELL HARBOR MARINA	
Area	Elliott Bay
Address	2203 Alaskan Way
Hours	All Hours
Length of Stay	Hourly, Day, and Overnight Rates
Tie Up Space	Approximately 40 slips
Suitable For	Yachts, Cruiser, Runabouts
Type	Public, Port of Seattle
Contact	(206) 615-3952 or (206) 615-3953 Channel 66 A on your VHF
Fuel	No
Insider Tips	Contact Guard to let you through the marina's gate when returning to your boat.

ELLIOTT BAY

Bell Harbor Marina

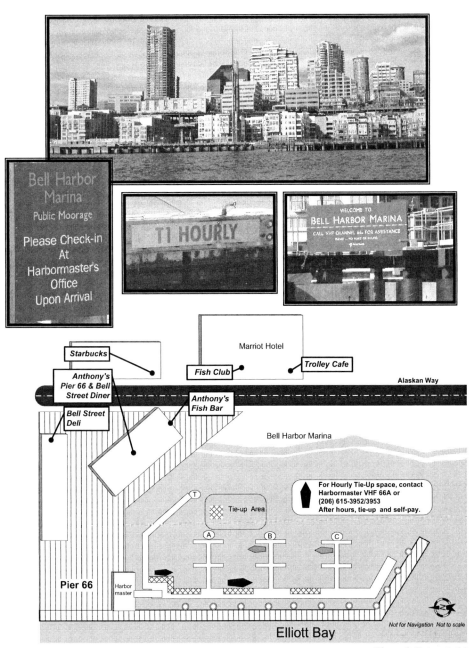

Bell Harbor
Marina
Public Moorage
Please Check-in
At
Harbormaster's
Office
Upon Arrival

T1 HOURLY

WELCOME TO
BELL HARBOR MARINA
CALL VHF CHANNEL 66A FOR ASSISTANCE

Marriot Hotel

Starbucks

Fish Club

Trolley Cafe

Alaskan Way

Anthony's Pier 66 & Bell Street Diner

Anthony's Fish Bar

Bell Street Deli

Bell Harbor Marina

T

Tie-up Area

For Hourly Tie-Up space, contact Harbormaster VHF 66A or (206) 615-3952/3953
After hours, tie-up and self-pay.

A

B

C

Pier 66

Harbor master

Not for Navigation Not to scale

Elliott Bay

ELLIOTT BAY
Bell Harbor Marina

ANTHONY'S PIER 66 & BELL STREET DINER

Anthony's Pier 66 serves fresh seasonal Northwest seafood dishes and is one of the nicest and most modern of Anthony's 18 waterfront locations in the greater Puget Sound area. Dungeness Crab is a highlight, including the crab cocktail, crab chowder, and crab salad. A favorite seafood dish is the "Potlatch" with steamed clams, fresh local mussels, split steamed Alaskan crab legs, and fresh oysters on the half shell. The contemporary, sophisticated setting upstairs has a commanding view of the Seattle skyline, Mount Rainier, the Olympics and Elliott Bay. Anthony's high-energy Bell Street Diner downstairs features salmon burgers to char-grilled halibut on their all-day menu. Local produce and Northwest wines and microbrews complement the fresh Northwest seafood. The cozy bar and diner is a popular destination for business locals to unwind after a busy day. Anthony's is a privately held company owned by a Seattle native, Budd Gould.

Hours	Lunch: 11:30am – 3pm Daily Dinner (Downstairs): 3pm – 10pm Mon-Thur 3pm-10:30pm Fri-Sat 3pm-9pm Sundays Dinner (Upstairs): 5pm-9:30pm Mon-Thur 5pm-10pm Fri-Sat 5pm-9pm Sundays
Serving	Lunch, Dinner
Price	\$9 - \$24 Lunch \$16 - \$24 Dinner
Reservations	Recommended
Environment	Business Casual / Dressy
Outdoor Seating	Yes, Deck, Summer Months
Contact Info.	(206) 448-6680 Downstairs Diner (206) 448-6688 Upstairs Restaurant
Notables	❑ Next to Cruise Line Terminal

ANTHONY'S FISH BAR

This walk-up service fish 'n chips bar not only has great fish, but also offers indoor seating and plenty of outdoor deck seating with a wonderful view of the Seattle skyline looking south towards the Mariners Stadium and the Seahawks Stadium. This Seattle waterfront location affords the casual visitor with a local seafood experience with a great view without paying the great view price. Starbucks coffee is available just across the street.

Hours	11am – 5pm Daily
Serving	Lunch, Dinner
Price	\$5 - \$10
Reservations	No
Cuisine	Seafood Fast Food
Environment	Casual
Outdoor Seating	Yes, Pier Deck, Summer Months
Contact Info.	(206) 448-6688

ELLIOTT BAY
Bell Harbor Marina

BELL STREET DELI

The Bell Street Deli, located at 2207 Alaskan Way just north of Pier 66, also serves as a small grocery with a selection of domestic, micro, and import beers for purchase. You can order specialty sandwiches or have the Deli make up your own sandwich creation. Tossed green salads are also available. The Bell Street Deli breakfast sandwich consists of an English muffin with egg, cheese, and your choice of sausage or bacon.

Hours	7:30am - 7pm Mon-Sat
Serving	Breakfast, Lunch, Dinner
Price	$5 - $10
Reservations	No
Cuisine	Sandwiches, Salads
Environment	Casual
Outdoor Seating	No
Contact Info.	(206) 441-6907

FISH CLUB

The Fish Club is located in the Marriott Hotel at 2100 Alaskan Way. This spacious restaurant and bar with its tile floor and modern décor has a New York look and feel with an excellent seafood menu drawn from coastal cultures around the world. For starters, try the Mediterranean plate with hummus, caponata and zesty tapanade with grilled pita bread and feta cheese. For the sea plate, the Pacific cod with polenta, Maitaki mushroom ragu, braised rapini, and shaved Oregon truffles is a nice choice. Soups and chowders like the authentic Louisiana seafood gumbo and salads like the fish club Caesar are also specialties at the Fish Club. Roasted chicken, beef tenderloin, and lamb are additional tasty choices on the menu. The Fish Club also offers hand-crafted specialty drinks and classic cocktails.

Hours	Lunch: 11:30am – 2:30pm Daily Dinner: 5pm – 10pm Sun-Thur 5pm – 11pm Fri & Sat Brunch: 6:30am – 2:30pm Sat-Sun
Serving	Lunch, Dinner, Brunch
Price	$7 - $12 Lunch $12 - $28 Dinner $20 Brunch
Reservations	Recommended
Environment	Business Casual / Dressy
Outdoor Seating	No
Contact Info.	(206) 256-1040

ELLIOTT BAY
Bell Harbor Marina

STARBUCKS

This Starbucks is worth pointing out because of its convenient location next to Bell Harbor and the waterfront trolley with access to the Seattle waterfront shops and other restaurants. Starbucks began in Seattle and opened its first shop at Pike Place Market in 1971. Starbucks continues to be a favorite in the Pacific Northwest and is a quick alternative for boaters looking for a good cup of coffee and some sweet treats.

Hours	5:30am – 5:30pm Mon-Fri 6:30am – 5:30pm Sat & Sun Winter Hours Vary
Serving	Coffee, Cookies, Pastries
Price	$3 - $8
Reservations	No
Cuisine	Coffee, Cookies, Pastries
Environment	Casual
Outdoor Seating	Yes, Sidewalk, Summer Months
Contact Info.	(206) 448-9304

THE TROLLEY CAFE

The Trolley Café is located in the new Marriott Hotel on the south end of the building complex. This small café offers sandwiches, salads, fruit-cups, ice cream, chips, and soft drinks. The Café also sells beer, wine, books, magazines, and gift items. Outdoor seating is available during the summer months.

Hours	6:30am – 10pm Daily Closing Hours Vary
Serving	Sandwiches, Salads
Price	$3-$7
Reservations	No
Outdoor Seating	Yes, Patio, Summer Months
Contact Info.	(206) 256-1147

ELLIOTT BAY
Bell Harbor Marina

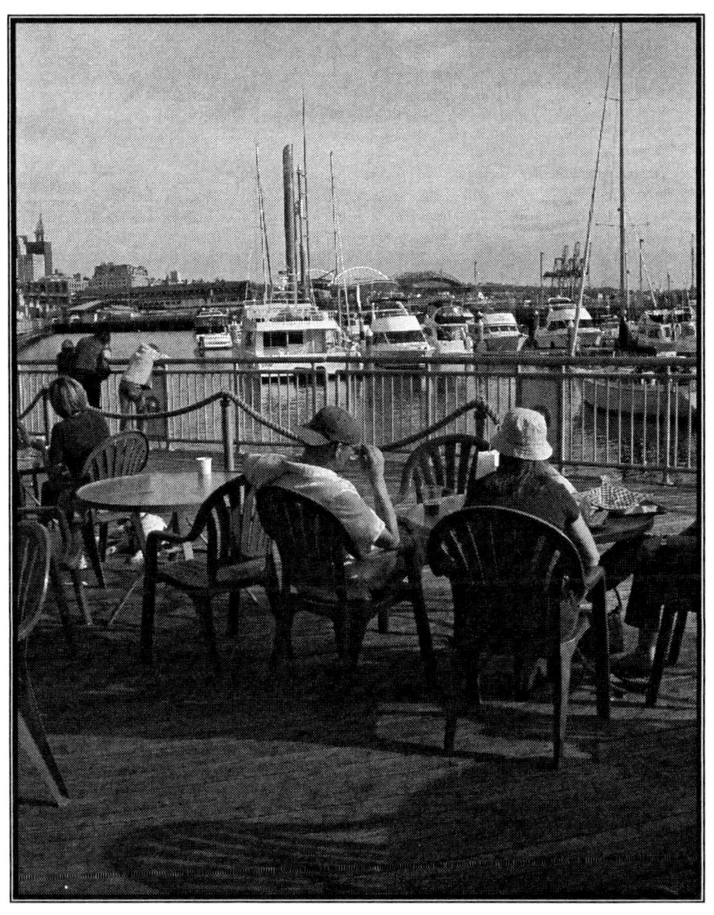

<u>ELLIOTT BAY</u>

Elliott Bay Marina

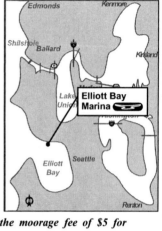

Elliott Bay Marina began construction in 1989 and was completed in 1991 after meeting stringent environmental guidelines. One of the largest marinas in the Seattle area, Elliott Bay Marina has 1,200 slips ranging in size from 32 feet to 63 feet. There are also pier ends that are able to accommodate virtually any sized pleasure craft. This location has three great restaurants from which to choose.

To secure a space at the Marina for dining purposes, call the Marina ahead of your expected arrival time, and they will assign you to a slip or direct you to available tie-up space. After disembarking, check in at the Marina's Office located below the Palisade Restaurant to pay the moorage fee of $5 for 3 hours (vessels over 46 feet $10).

RESTAURANTS
Maggie Bluffs
Palisade

Day and overnight rates run $1 per foot ($1.50 for vessels over 46 feet) with an additional $3 charge for power hook-up. You can find fuel and pump out facilities at the end of the "G" dock. For long-term stays, boaters may make use of the showers, restrooms, and laundry facilities. There are also slip-side pump outs.

The 24-hour intercom security system allows you to return to your boat by checking in with security at the gate through the intercom system. The Marina Office is open 24hrs a day.

ELLIOTT BAY MARINA	
Area	Elliott Bay
Address	2601 West Marina Place
Hours	All Hours
Length of Stay	Hourly Rates and Overnight Rates
Tie Up Space	Available Slips or Slips Not Leased
Suitable For	Yachts, Cruiser, Runabouts
Type	Private, Elliott Bay Marina
Contact	(206) 285-4817 Channel 78 A on your VHF
Fuel	Yes, "G" Dock
Launch	No
Insider Tips	❑ Full During 4th of July ❑ Full New Year's Eve

ELLIOTT BAY
Elliott Bay Marina

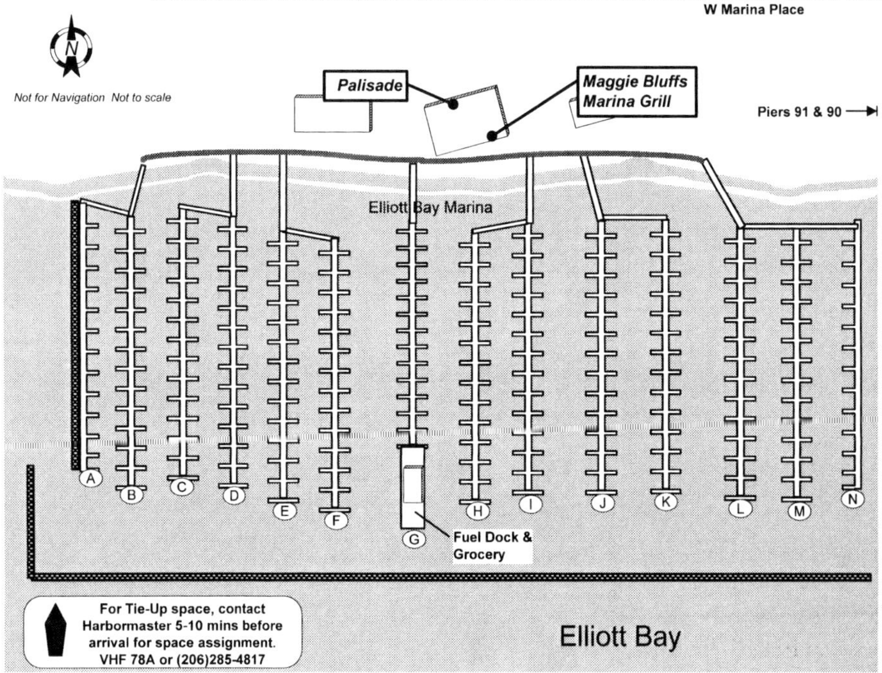

ELLIOTT BAY

Elliott Bay Marina

MAGGIE BLUFF'S CAFE

This cozy, casual café with wood paneling and tile/wood floors is an intimate and friendly café that is popular among the locals since it is off the beaten path for most tourists by car. The view is superb, looking southeast across Elliott Bay towards the Space Needle and the Seattle skyline. The menu is varied and includes a wide selection of sandwiches, burgers, and garden salads. Try the Crisp Greens salad with creamy Maytag blue cheese, toasted almonds, hard-cooked egg, and sweet bay shrimp. On colder days, enjoy the prime rib chili or the grill clam chowder or one of their hearty noodle dishes like the Salmon Soba. There is a full service bar with onion rings, shoestring fries, chicken wings, and other "finger food for friends."

Hours	Breakfast: 9am - 11am Sat & Sun Lunch/Dinner: 11am - 9pm Mon-Thur 11am – 9:30pm Fri & Sat Sunday Summers
Serving	Breakfast, Lunch, Dinner
Price	$7-$15 Lunch/Dinner
Reservations	Recommended, summer months
Cuisine	Burgers, Salads, Sandwiches
Environment	Casual
Outdoor Seating	Yes, Patio, Summer Months
Contact Info.	(206) 283-8322

PALISADE

The Palisade Restaurant is above the Marina Office and has a panoramic view of downtown Seattle, the Space Needle, Mount Rainier, and the Olympic Mountains not to mention the boating activity of Elliott Bay. Getting to your table can be an adventure in itself as you cross a bridge suspended over a saltwater tide pool with live fish. The warm woods add to the nautical feel of this spacious restaurant including the large bar, which stays open 2 hours after the last dinner seating. The Palisade features fresh seafood cuisine combining Pacific and Polynesian influences. Live crab, lobster, cedar plank salmon, prime rib and other dishes are prepared in specialty ovens and grills. Desserts include the Polynesian chocolate fondue, seasonal fruit crisp, and the spiced banana ice cream sundae.

Hours	Brunch: 10am - 2pm Sundays Dinner: 5pm - 9pm Mon-Thur 5pm - 10pm Fridays 4pm - 10pm Saturdays 4:30pm - 9pm Sundays
Serving	Brunch, Dinner
Price	$18-$23 Brunch $20-$60 Dinner
Reservations	Recommended
Cuisine	Seafood, Prime Rib
Environment	Business Casual / Dressy
Outdoor Seating	Yes, Deck off the Lounge
Contact Info.	(206) 285-1000

ELLIOTT BAY
Elliott Bay Marina

ELLIOTT BAY

Seacrest Park

This City of Seattle dock and park possess the most stupendous view of the Seattle skyline, including the Cascade Mountains, Mt. Rainier, Mt. Baker, and the marine activity of Elliott Bay.

An L-shaped floating dock located to the shore side of a high fishing pier offers boaters tie-up space on the inside of the float and a couple of spaces on the outside of the float. The base of the L-shaped float is reserved for boats rented through the Alki Crab & Fish Company. Tbe south end, beach side of the L float/dock is reserved for the Alki-to-Seattle water taxi, which operates April to Labor Day. Both reserved areas are marked on the float/dock. The remainder of the float is available to the public for a 2-hour tie-up. The guest/taxi float is removed during the winter months and is normally available for use May through September or until early October.

Seacrest Park and the surrounding area is a popular scuba diving location; and the fishing pier is populated with pole & line folks so be careful when arriving and departing.

RESTAURANTS
Alki Crab & Fish Co.
Bubbles
Salty's
Thai on Alki

SEACREST PARK	
Area	Elliott Bay
Address	1660 Harbor Ave. SW, Seattle
Hours	All Hours
Length of Stay	2 Hours
Tie Up Space	100 feet, approximately
Suitable For	Yachts, Cruiser, Runabouts
Type	Public, City of Seattle Parks Dept.
Contact	(206) 684-4075
Fuel	No
Launch	North of Park (Don Armeni Boat Ramp)
Insider Tips	❑ Guest float available May-Sept. ❑ Beware of fishing lines ❑ Make way for the Water Taxi ❑ Scuba Divers may be present

ELLIOTT BAY

Seacrest Park

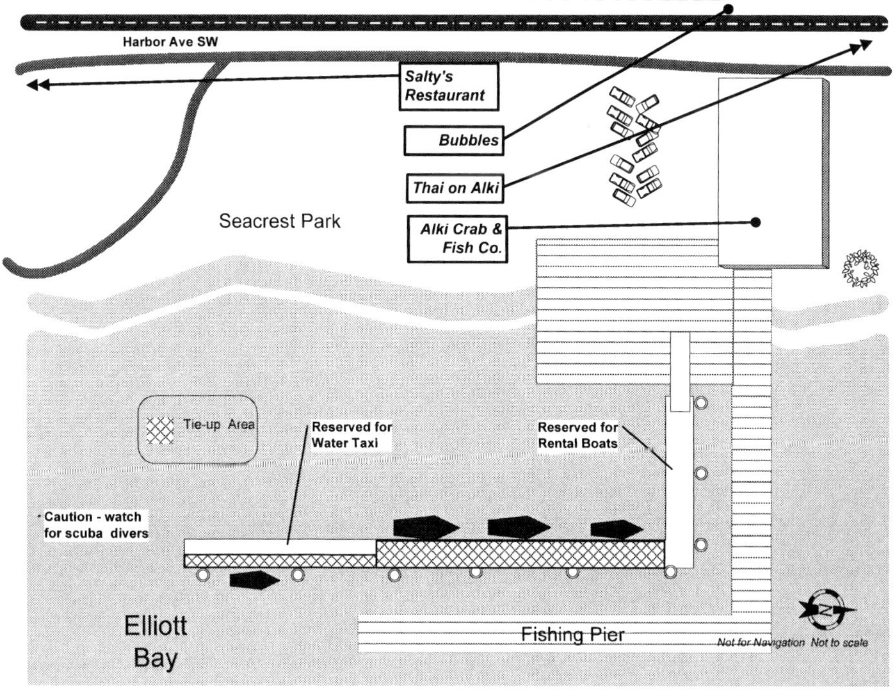

Harbor Ave SW

Salty's Restaurant

Bubbles

Thai on Alki

Alki Crab & Fish Co.

Seacrest Park

Tie-up Area

Reserved for Water Taxi

Reserved for Rental Boats

Caution - watch for scuba divers

Elliott Bay

Fishing Pier

Not for Navigation Not to scale

ELLIOTT BAY
Seacrest Park

ALKI CRAB & FISH CO.

The Alki Crab & Fish Co. is located at The City of Seattle Seacrest Park. The Park with its wonderful view makes this Café a great place to relax with some good fish 'n chips, shrimp and crab cocktails, or a platter of oysters, scallops, and prawns. Manila Clams in butter sauce is also available in season. This small country style cafe has cozy seating inside or you can enjoy one of the picnic tables in the Park. The Café also operates a rental shop for fishing, kayaking, boating, and bicycling. A great way to discover the beautiful beaches of Alki Point, where the first pioneers of Seattle landed in 1851, is to tour this area by bike. Bicycle rentals run $7 per hour from the Alki Crab & Fish Co. Rentals, including in-line skates, are available on sunny days during the summers from 11am to 6pm. Call 206-953-0237 for reservations.

Hours	Lunch/Dinner: 10am – 6:30pm Mon-Thur 9am – 8pm Fri-Sat 9am – 6:30pm Sundays Winter Hours Vary
Serving	Lunch, Dinner
Price	$4-$10
Reservations	No
Environment	Casual
Outdoor Seating	Yes, Picnic Benches
Contact Info.	(206) 938-0975
Notables	❑ Bicycle Rentals ❑ Fishing Rentals & Licenses ❑ Boat & Kayak Rentals ❑ Water Taxi April -Labor Day

BUBBLES

This small, charming espresso shop offers boaters drip coffee, espresso drinks, "bubble teas," gelato, fresh baked pastries, and Vietnamese baguette sandwiches. There are chairs of every size and comfort for one to sit and read the local newspapers and magazines. Bubbles is located directly across from Seacrest Park and is a nice place to relax and enjoy a special treat with water views of Seattle.

Hours	6am – 6pm Mon-Fri 8am – 8pm Saturdays 8am – 7pm Sundays
Serving	Coffee, Pastries, Sandwiches
Price	$2-$5
Reservations	No
Environment	Casual
Outdoor Seating	No
Contact Info.	(206) 938-0153

THAI ON ALKI

The Thai on Alki is located north of Seacrest Park and across the street from the Don Armeni Boat Ramp. For the lover of Thai cuisine, this is a great stop with friendly service and an extensive menu of authentic Thai dishes. Trout Chue Chee, Thai Prawn, Ginger Beef, and Pad Thai Chicken are just a few of the many dishes offered at this family run restaurant. Mild and medium dishes are available as well as hot and extra hot spicy dishes.

Hours	Lunch/Dinner: 11:30am-3pm and 5pm-10pm Mon-Fri 11:30am-10pm Sat & Sun
Serving	Lunch, Dinner
Price	$7-$15
Reservations	Accepted
Environment	Casual
Outdoor Seating	No
Contact Info.	(206) 938-2992

SALTY'S

Salty's is located just south and within walking distance of Seacrest Park. Salty's commands the same incredible panoramic view, as does the Park. This restaurant has plenty of windows, patios, and decks from which to observe the ferry traffic, the barges and tugs, freighters, and pleasure boats. Salty's completes the ambiance with its nautical décor of fishing rods and a cozy fireplace. The extensive menu includes salmon, oysters, clams, prawns, and live crab and lobster. The seafood dishes are complemented with pasta, chicken, and char-broiled steaks. Friday and Monday nights at Salty's are especially fun with live jazz from 9 pm to midnight. The Sunday Brunch buffet is outstanding and includes a variety of meats, seafood, fruits, crepes, omelets, and Eggs Benedict just to name a few of the many choices. Salty's has been a Seattle icon for many years and continues to maintain its popularity with locals and tourists alike.

Hours	Brunch: 9am - 2pm Sundays And 9:45am – 2:45pm Saturdays May-Aug Lunch: 11am - 2:30pm Mon-Fri 11:30am - 3pm Sat Dinner: 5pm - 10pm Mon-Thur 5pm – 11 pm Fridays 4pm – 11 pm Sat 4pm – 10 pm Sundays Winter Hours: Close at 9pm Sun-Thur Close at 9:30pm Fri & Sat
Serving	Brunch, Lunch, Dinner
Price	$28 Brunch $10-$40 Lunch $23-$40 Dinner
Reservations	Recommended
Environment	Casual / Business Casual / Dressy
Outdoor Seating	Yes, "Wraparound Deck" and "Seaside Patio"
Contact Info.	(206) 937-1600 www.saltys.com

ELLIOTT BAY
Washington Street Dock

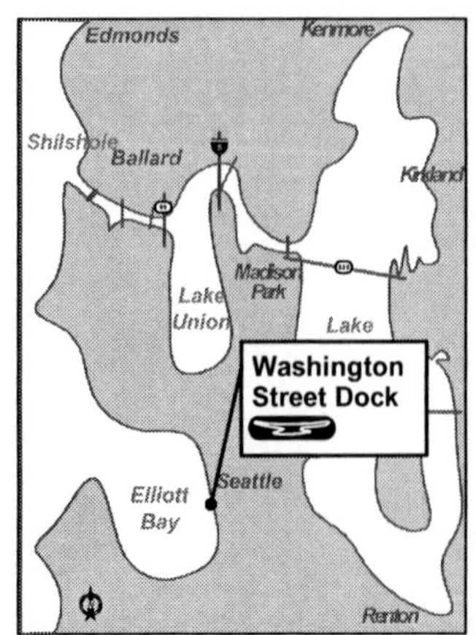

CLOSED

This historic public boat landing is currently not available to boaters. The dock was destroyed in a winter storm and the seawall along the adjacent park has given way. The City of Seattle has been in the process of obtaining funding to restore the park and build a new dock. This location was a popular tie-up space for boaters attending the Seattle Seahawk and Mariner games. Plans for development of this location are currently on hold pending the outcome of the replacement of the Alaskan Way Viaduct road system.

The hand-made iron pergola at this site was built in 1920 and is on the National Register of Historic Places. This site has fulfilled a number of uses, including a landing for ferries and ocean-going ships, the headquarters of the Seattle Harbor Patrol, and as the U.S. Navy's official shore-leave landing and departure point.

The City of Seattle would appreciate your support and encouragement to continue efforts to restore this historic site and dock.

WASHINGTON STREET DOCK		
	Area	Elliott Bay
	Address	S. Washington Street
	Hours	CURRENTLY CLOSED
	Length of Stay	
	Tie Up Space	CURRENTLY CLOSED
	Suitable For	
	Type	City of Seattle Parks Dept.
	Contact	(206) 684-7249
	Fuel	No
	Launch	No
	Insider Tips	❑ Encourage the City to continue its efforts to restore this historic site

ELLIOTT BAY
Washington Street Dock

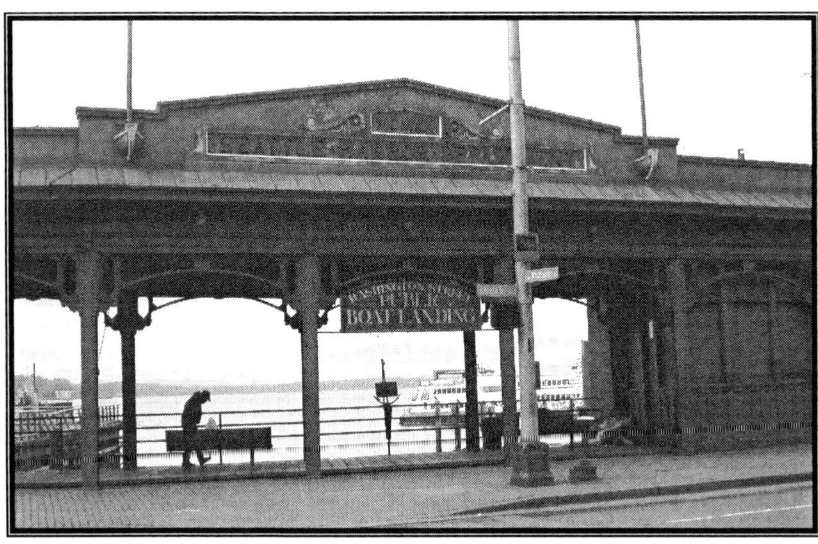

Lake Washington

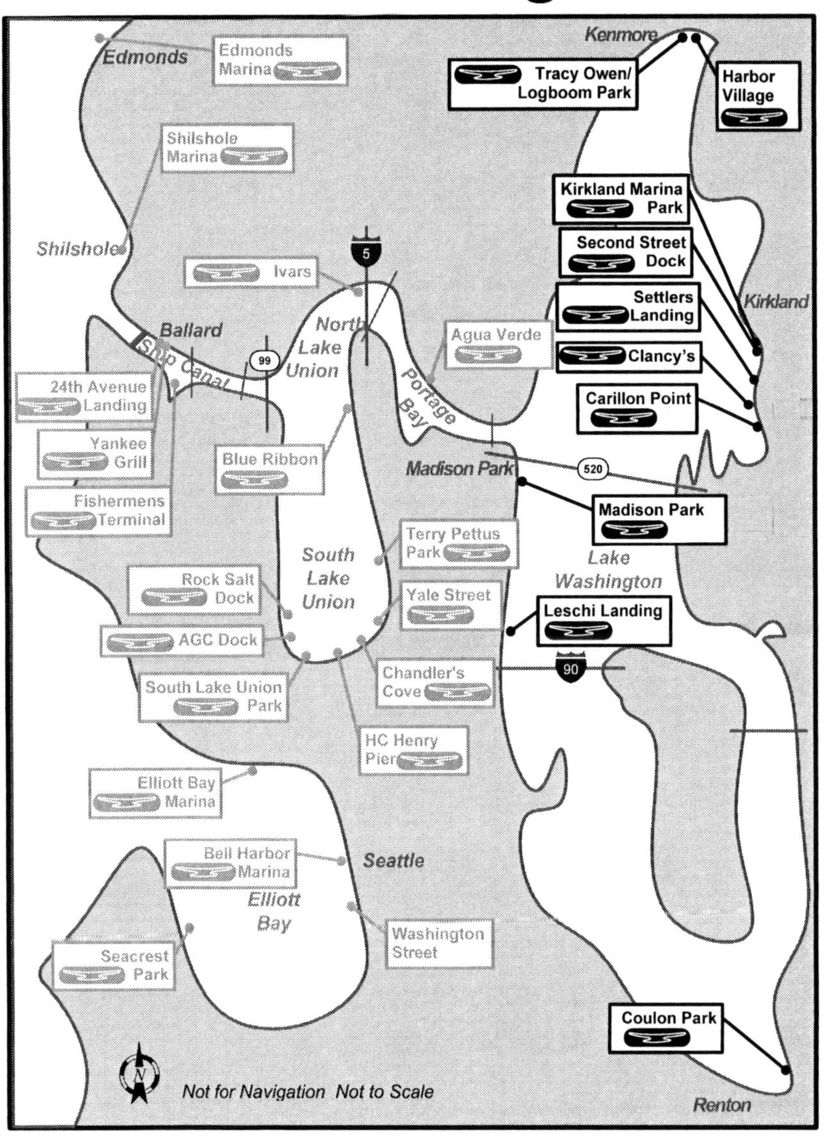
Edmonds
Edmonds Marina
Kenmore
Tracy Owen/ Logboom Park
Harbor Village
Shilshole Marina
Kirkland Marina Park
Second Street Dock
Shilshole
Ivars
5
Settlers Landing
Kirkland
Ballard
Ship Canal
North Lake Union
99
Agua Verde
Clancy's
24th Avenue Landing
Portage Bay
Carillon Point
Yankee Grill
Blue Ribbon
Madison Park
520
Fishermens Terminal
Madison Park
Terry Pettus Park
South Lake Union
Lake Washington
Rock Salt Dock
Yale Street
Leschi Landing
AGC Dock
90
Chandler's Cove
South Lake Union Park
HC Henry Pier
Elliott Bay Marina
Bell Harbor Marina
Seattle
Elliott Bay
Washington Street
Seacrest Park
Coulon Park
Not for Navigation Not to Scale
Renton

KENMORE

Harbor Village Marina

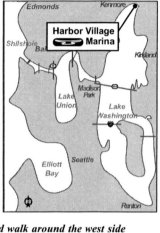

Guests of the Roaster & Taproom restaurant are invited to use the guest tie-up area located on the outside of the breakwater of the Harbor Village Marina.

With ample room along the breakwater pier, there's rarely a problem finding space to tie-up here. In addition, the Kenmore Tracy Owen/Logboom public pier will definitely have space available and is just next door to the west. The north end of Lake Washington, Kenmore area, is normally calm, so wave and wake action shouldn't be a big problem.

RESTAURANT	Roaster & Taproom

Once you are tied-up along the breakwater pier at the Harbor Village Marina, it's a short walk through the gate up the main dock; keep to the left and walk around the west side of the building to the restaurant entrance.

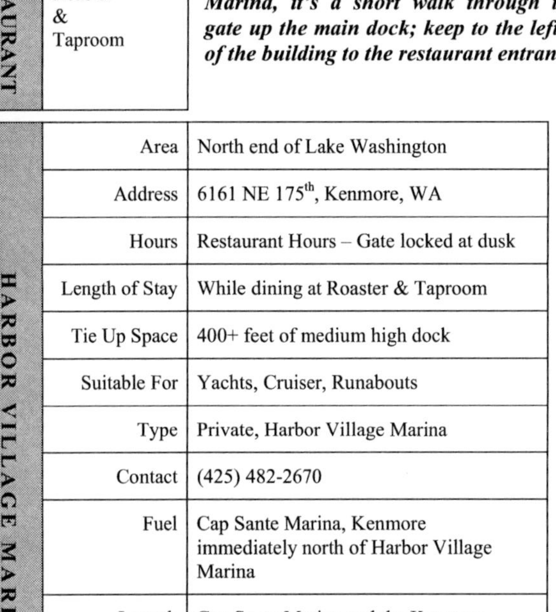

HARBOR VILLAGE MARINA		
	Area	North end of Lake Washington
	Address	6161 NE 175th, Kenmore, WA
	Hours	Restaurant Hours – Gate locked at dusk
	Length of Stay	While dining at Roaster & Taproom
	Tie Up Space	400+ feet of medium high dock
	Suitable For	Yachts, Cruiser, Runabouts
	Type	Private, Harbor Village Marina
	Contact	(425) 482-2670
	Fuel	Cap Sante Marina, Kenmore immediately north of Harbor Village Marina
	Launch	Cap Sante Marina and the Kenmore Sammamish River Boat Launch
	Insider Tips	❑ Gate at head of main dock is closed and locked at DUSK ❑ Shallow water to the east of the marked channel – Stay in the marked channel

NOTE: The gate at the head of the main dock is closed and locked at dusk. If you are returning to your boat after dusk, you will need to ask the restaurant personnel to open the gate.

KENMORE
Harbor Village Marina

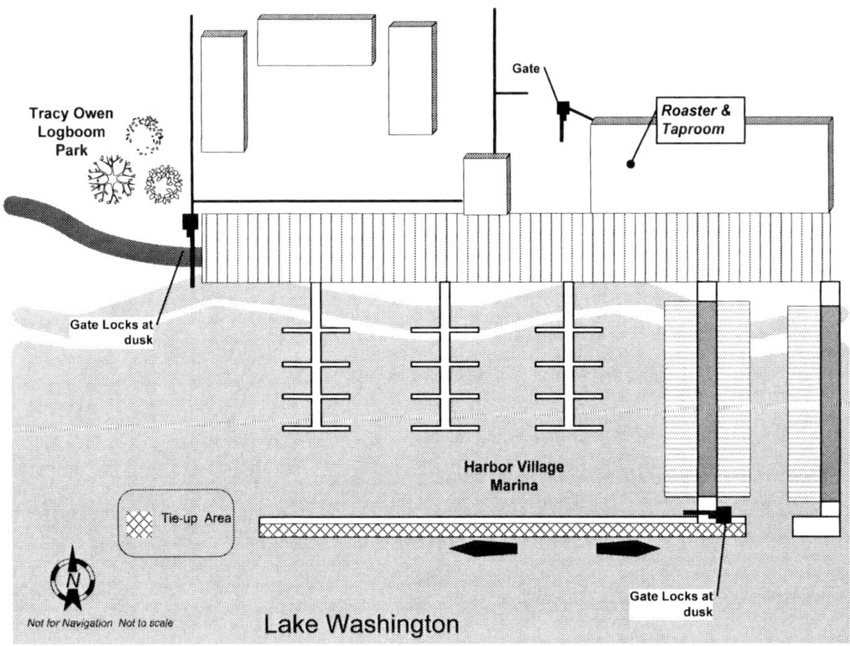

KENMORE
Harbor Village Marina

ROASTER & TAPROOM RESTAURANT

A fun, lively eatery during all seasons, this restaurant is divided into two main areas. The dining area, the Roaster, has ample seating for all ages, including window seating overlooking the Harbor Village Marina and the Kenmore Harbor. The menu specializes in slow-roasted meats including pork, chicken, turkey and prime rib. Try the fruitwood smoked turkey served with orange-cranberry relish, garlic-mashed potatoes with scratch turkey gravy, and fresh vegetables with lemon butter. A children's menu is also available. The alehouse area, the Taproom, provides outdoor seating for warm weather dining with a nice selection of roasted sandwiches and salads. The Taproom is popular for its large selection of single-malt scotches, small-batch bourbons, and draft beers and provides big screen TV's for watching sporting events.

Note: The gate to the Harbor Village Marina is locked at dusk. When arriving by boat after dusk, phone the number posted on the gate and restaurant personnel will escort you to and from your boat.

Hours	Lunch: 11:30am – 4pm Daily Dinner: 4pm – 10pm Daily Taproom: open till Midnight 11 pm Sun & Mon
Serving	Lunch, Dinner
Price	$5 - $10 Lunch $10 - $20 Dinner
Reservations	Recommended
Environment	Business Casual
Outdoor Seating	Yes, Limited Patio Space
Contact Info.	(425) 482-2670 www.restaurants.com
Notables	❑ Call Number at Gate ❑ Special Event Nights

Have an alternative
when the moorage is full.

KENMORE

Harbor Village Marina

KENMORE

Tracy Owen/Logboom Park

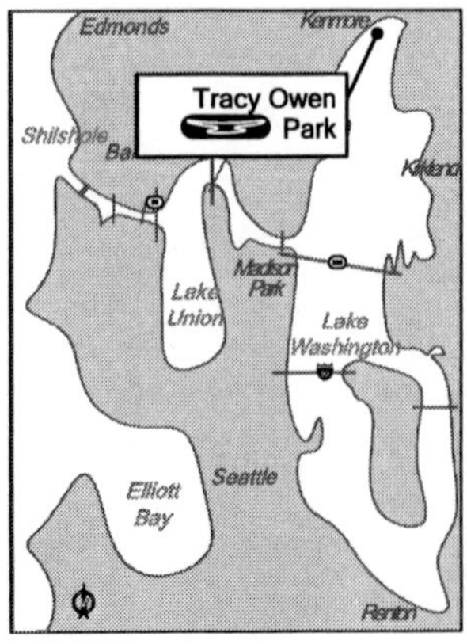

This City of Kenmore park and public pier is located at the north end of Lake Washington; and although it is an excellent facility with plenty of day moorage, it sees very little use by boaters so space is most always available. The public dock serves as an alternative guest space when the Harbor Village Marina guest space is full. The Roaster & Taproom restaurant is within easy walking distance of the Tracy Owen public dock.

RESTAURANT
Roaster & Taproom

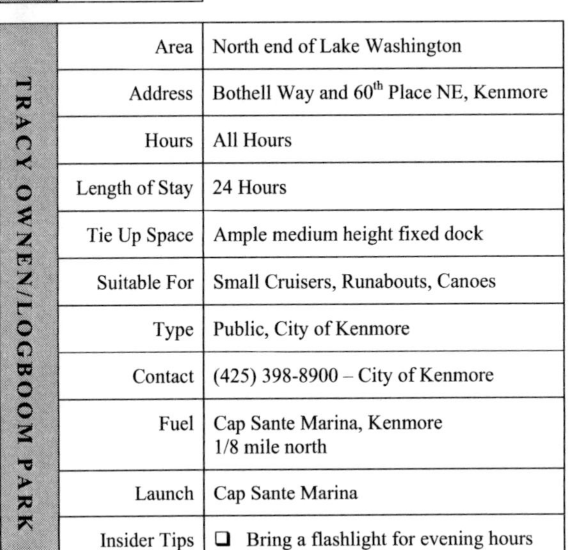

TRACY OWNEN/LOGBOOM PARK

Area	North end of Lake Washington
Address	Bothell Way and 60th Place NE, Kenmore
Hours	All Hours
Length of Stay	24 Hours
Tie Up Space	Ample medium height fixed dock
Suitable For	Small Cruisers, Runabouts, Canoes
Type	Public, City of Kenmore
Contact	(425) 398-8900 – City of Kenmore
Fuel	Cap Sante Marina, Kenmore 1/8 mile north
Launch	Cap Sante Marina
Insider Tips	❑ Bring a flashlight for evening hours ❑ Dock often not clean

KENMORE
Tracy Owen/Logboom Park

State Route 522

Burke-Gilman Trail

NE 175th Street

Gate

Not for Navigation
Not to scale

Gate Locks at dusk

Cap Sante Marina

Kenmore Air

Tracy Owen Logboom Park

Harbor Village Marina

Roaster & Taproom

Tie-up Area

Lake Washington

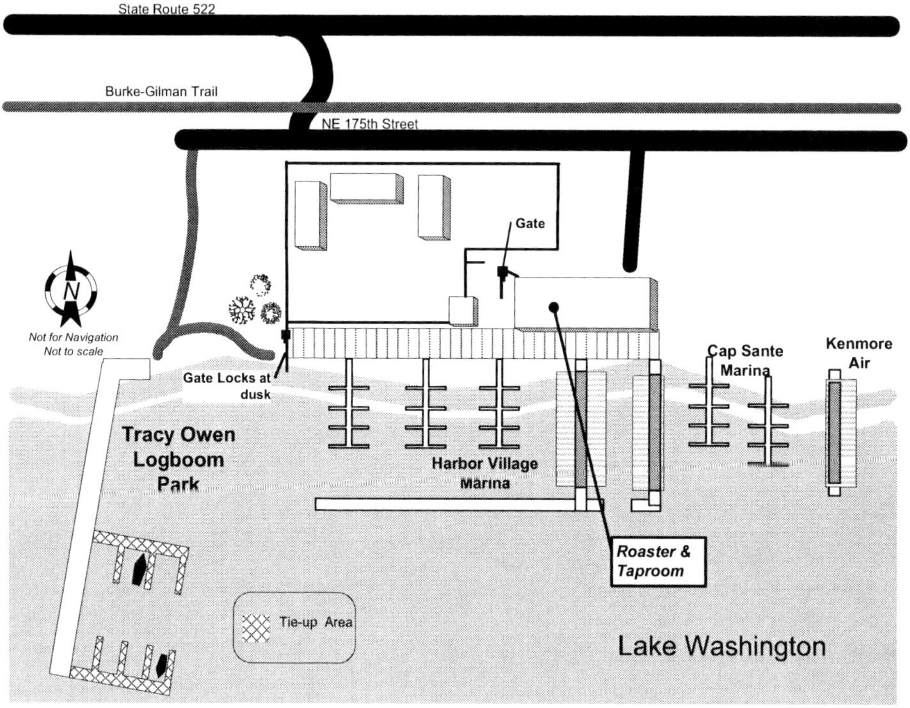

KIRKLAND

Carillon Point Guest Dock

Once a ship building yard and later the training facility for the Seattle Seahawks, Carillon Point is now an upscale development offering facilities for boaters with excellent tie-ups for almost every class of watercraft. Located on the eastern shore of Lake Washington between the cities of Kirkland and Bellevue, Carillon provides a great place to sit and relax, listen to the Carillon chimes, or stroll along the promenade.

Five restaurants and a coffee shop ranging from casual to formal await boaters and are within easy walking distance from the Carillon Point dock. Carillon also offers the boating visitor a selection of retail shops, a spa, Starbucks, and a post office. The Woodmark Hotel offers visitors to Carillon Point some of the area's finest accommodations. The neighboring Yarrow Bay Marina has fuel, marine supplies, marine services, and boat rentals. Boaters can find nearly everything at Carillon Point.

RESTAURANTS
Beach Cafe
Cucina Cucina
Popinjays Café
Starbucks Coffee
Waters Bistro
Yarrow Bay Grill

CARILLON POINT GUEST DOCK	
Area	East Shore of Lake Washington south of Kirkland
Address	Carillon Point, Kirkland
Hours	All Hours
Length of Stay	2 hours
Tie Up Space	Approximately 150 Feet
Suitable For	Yachts, Cruisers, Runabouts, Canoes
Type	Private, Carillon Point Properties
Contact	(425) 822-1700
Fuel	Yarrow Bay Marina
Launch	Yarrow Bay Marina
Insider Tips	❑ Professionals help with lines during the summer months ❑ Boats under 32' inside and larger outside of breakwater ❑ STARBOARD tie ❑ Boat Rentals at Yarrow Bay Marina

KIRKLAND

Carillon Point Guest Dock

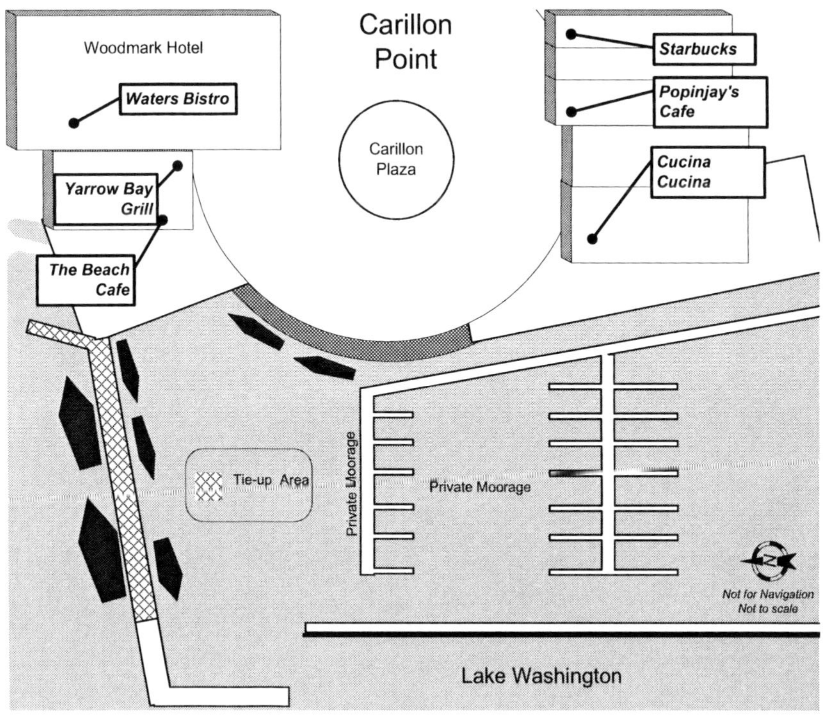

KIRKLAND

Carillon Point Guest Dock

THE BEACH CAFE

The Beach Café has a fresh, lively fare with five different specials offered every day along with delicious soups and sandwiches. The menu includes flavors from the Southwest, Tuscany, and Caribbean spices as well as Northwest traditions. The prawn linguine made with white gulf prawns, artichoke hearts, spinach, smoked tomato-thyme vodka sauce, fresh linguine with asiago cheese is just one example of the award winning dishes. Fine wines and good local micro brews are available for lunch and dinner and the Café has a full service bar. This art deco café is especially busy in the summer months when the lakeside patio is open for seating with great views of Lake Washington and the Olympic Mountains.

Hours	Lunch: 11am - 5 pm Daily Dinner: 5pm - 10 pm Mon-Sat 5pm - 9 pm Sundays Summers: Open till 10 pm Week-Days and 11 pm Week-Ends
Serving	Lunch, Dinner
Price	$9 - $17 Lunch $12 - $20 Dinner
Reservations	Recommended
Environment	Business Casual
Outdoor Seating	Yes, Patio, Summers
Contact Info.	(425) 889-0303 www.ybbeachcafe.com
Notables	❑ Daily Specials ❑ Happy Hr. Specials

CUCINA CUCINA

Started in Seattle, Cucina Cucina has restaurants throughout the Northwest and offers Seattle area boaters a waterfront location. Cucina's at Carillon Point offers diner's excellent views to the west of Lake Washington and Yarrow Point. A high-energy restaurant for all ages, Cucina serves great Italian pizzas, pastas, and salads and also offers steak and seafood dishes. The stone oven, very thin pizzas are especially good and so are the classic Italian pasta dishes. Dishes are designed and presented so you can share with others in your party. Be sure to try the new-age drinks, which are also available in the bar. The bar stays open 30 to 45 minutes longer than the restaurant on most nights.

Hours	Lunch: 11:30am – 4pm Mon-Sat Noon – 4pm Sundays Dinner: 4pm - 9 pm Sun-Thur 4pm - 10 pm Fri & Sat
Serving	Lunch, Dinner
Price	$8 - $16 Lunch $13 - $19 Dinner
Reservations	Phone-Ahead-Program (30-45 min.) (placed on waiting list)
Environment	Business Casual
Outdoor Seating	Year-round Heated Covered Area
Contact Info.	(425) 822-4000 www.cucinacucina.com
Notables	❑ Daily Fish Special ❑ Special Birthday Song

KIRKLAND
Carillon Point Guest Dock

POPPINJAY'S CAFE

This family owned and operated café and catering business prepares gourmet sandwiches, salads, and soups popular with the professional and tourist alike. You will find lines during the lunch hour at this popular stop. Favorites include the turkey crème cheese cranberry sandwich and the chicken salad sandwich. Daily soup and sandwich specials are written on the deli board. Don't miss the Wisconsin Cheese soup, another tasty favorite. This casual upscale delicatessen provides outdoor seating to enjoy that hot cup of espresso and scrumptious sweets or that classic frozen yogurt with fruit. If you are looking for a breakfast venue, don't forget Poppinjay's, serving up omelets, scrambled eggs, and a variety of pastries.

Hours	Breakfast: 7am - 10am Mon-Fri Lunch: 10am - 4pm Mon-Fri
Serving	Breakfast, Lunch
Price	$4-$6 Breakfast $7-$10 Lunch
Reservations	No
Environment	Casual
Outdoor Seating	Yes, Patio, Summer Months
Contact Info.	(425) 828-3048 www.carillon-point.com
Notables	❑ Full Catering Service ❑ Nautical Shopping Next Door

KIRKLAND
Carillon Point Guest Dock

WATERS BISTRO

The Waters Bistro is located within the prestigious Four Star Woodmark Hotel. The menu consists of Northwest cuisine with a Mediterranean accent and elegant presentation, including veal, chicken, seafood, and vegetarian dishes. For lunch, try the grilled chicken with parmesan risotto, asparagus, and basil. The dinner menu includes a roasted rack of lamb served with chickpea flan, roasted garlic, olives, oven-roasted tomato, and rosemary. The beverage selections emphasize west coast wines by the glass and Northwest ales. During the summer months, the patio is open for outside dining providing a majestic view of Lake Washington, the Olympics, and the Seattle skyline. Afternoon Tea is served in the cozy Library Bar at 2:30 pm, 3:00 pm, and 3:30 pm. Children are welcome and will enjoy their own special china and menu. Happy Hour is also available Monday through Friday from 5:00 pm to 7:00 pm. If you are looking for something extra special, the Waters Bistro at the Woodmark Hotel will sure to please.

Hours	Breakfast: 6:30am - 11am Mon-Fri 7am - 2pm Sat & Sun Lunch: 11:30am – 2pm Mon-Fri Dinner: 5pm - 9:30pm Daily
Serving	Breakfast, Lunch, Dinner
Price	$7-$15 Breakfast $8-$15 Lunch $6-$28 Dinner
Reservations	Recommended
Environment	Business Casual / Dressy
Outdoor Seating	Yes, Patio, Summer Months
Contact Info.	(425) 803-5595 www.watersbistro.com
Notables	❑ Sunday Brunch ❑ Afternoon Tea ❑ On-line Reservations ❑ Special Events

KIRKLAND

Carillon Point Guest Dock

YARROW BAY GRILL

The Yarrow Bay Grill is upstairs from The Beach Café in a more formal setting. The warm wood décor and fireplace makes this Grill a cozy intimate affair with a view from every table. The Yarrow Bay Grill has earned the reputation of being one of the best restaurants on the Eastside. And know wonder with dishes like the grilled Sea Bass with huckleberry port coulis, crispy sweet potato chips, and jasmine rice. Or the Muscovy Duck breast and Duck leg confit with dried cherry sauce and Yukon golds. The Yarrow Bay Grill has a commanding view of Lake Washington, the Seattle skyline, and the Olympic Mountains and offers pleasant outdoor patio dining during the summer months.

Hours	Dinner: 5:30pm – 9:30pm Mon-Thur 5:30pm – 10pm Fri & Sat 5pm - 9 pm Sundays Summers: Closing time extended ½ Hour
Serving	Dinner
Price	$18 - $39 Dinner
Reservations	Recommended
Cuisine	Seafood, Steak, Italian, Asian
Environment	Business Casual / Dressy
Outdoor Seating	Yes, Patio, Summer Months
Contact Info.	(425) 889-9052 www.ybbeachcafe.com

Make room for others, close gaps between boats.

KIRKLAND

Clancy's Foghorn Guest Dock

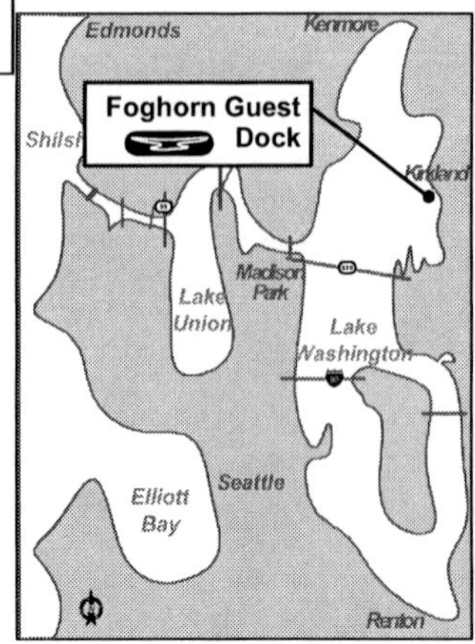

Clancy's Foghorn restaurant and guest dock is located between the city of Kirkland and Carillon Point. A nautical destination with ample space for boats can be found during most anytime of the year on this 120-foot dock belonging to Clancy's Bistro, formerly the Foghorn.

The only restaurant on the Eastside which has its very own dock makes this site a unique destination for boaters.

RESTAURANT
Clancy's Foghorn

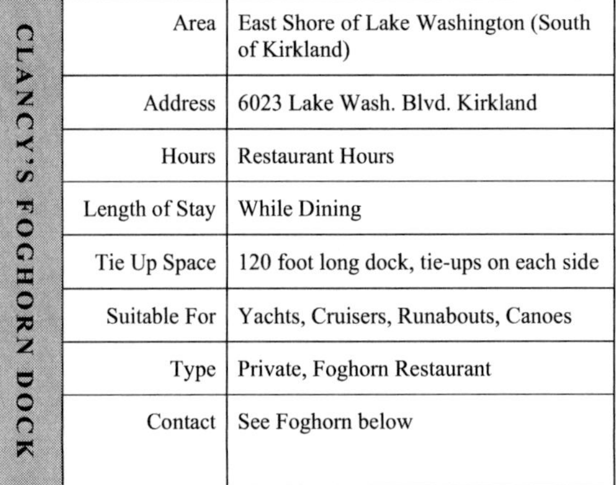

CLANCY'S FOGHORN DOCK	
Area	East Shore of Lake Washington (South of Kirkland)
Address	6023 Lake Wash. Blvd. Kirkland
Hours	Restaurant Hours
Length of Stay	While Dining
Tie Up Space	120 foot long dock, tie-ups on each side
Suitable For	Yachts, Cruisers, Runabouts, Canoes
Type	Private, Foghorn Restaurant
Contact	See Foghorn below

KIRKLAND
Clancy's Foghorn Guest Dock

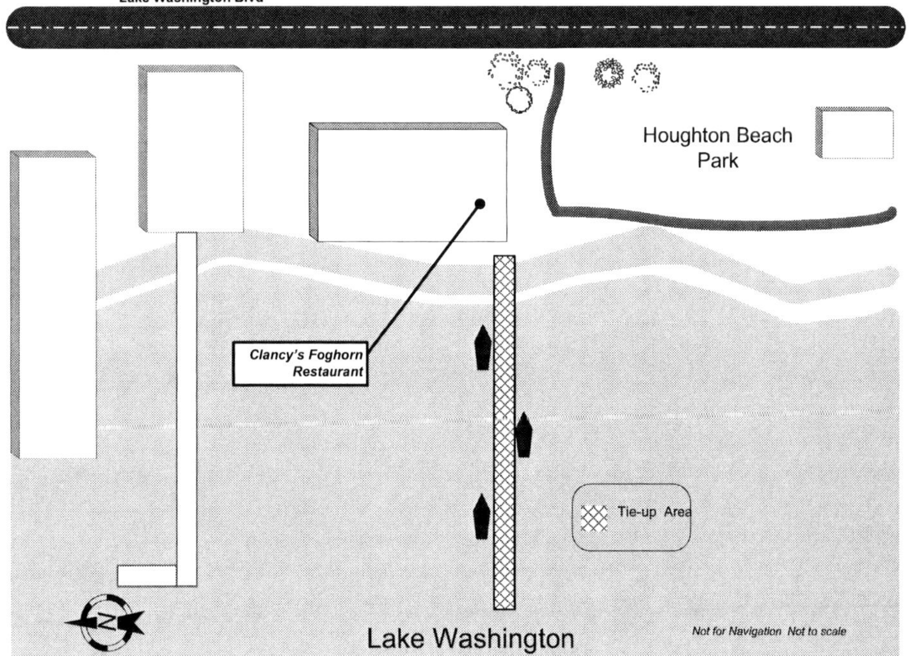

KIRKLAND
Clancy's Foghorn Guest Dock

CLANCY'S FOGHORN RESTAURANT

Tim Clancy, a former Seattle chef who has specialized in Italian cuisine for many years, recently purchased the former Foghorn Restaurant. Tim, a Kirkland resident, has brought a new bistro appeal to this restaurant venue with his expertise in Italian cuisine and the warm Italian atmosphere of linen set tables and fresh cut flowers. This romantic setting with its beautiful views of Lake Washington, the Olympic Mountains, and the Seattle skyline has been discovered by boaters as well, who frequent Clancy's guest dock.

Enjoy a glass of fine wine with a soup, salad, or antipasti starter like the Insalata di Spinaci with baby spinach, artichoke hearts, baked prosciutto and goat cheese or start with Bruschetta with fresh tomato and Roquefort cheese served on grilled como bread. For dinner try the veal medallions with capers and lemon or the fresh fish selection of the day. The pasta dishes are good too, including the Cannelloni di Vitella, fresh pasta tubes filled with veal, spinach, and ricotta baked in salsa rosa.

Hours	Dinner: 5pm – 10pm Mon-Sat 5pm – 9pm Sundays
Serving	Dinner
Price	$13 - $30
Reservations	Recommended
Cuisine	Chicken, Pasta, Seafood, Veal
Environment	Business Casual
Outdoor Seating	No
Contact Info.	(425) 827-0654

KIRKLAND

Clancy's Foghorn Guest Dock

KIRKLAND
Marina Park

The City of Kirkland public dock and Marina Park are unquestionably the best destination for hungry boaters. The city of Kirkland is a "happen'n place" with many art galleries, boutiques, and eateries all within a short walk of the public dock. The public dock offers extensive moorage and tie-up space for all types of watercraft for short term and multi-day stays with many slips, ranging in size from runabouts to yachts. The ends of the slip piers may also be used for moorage. Additionally, there is a 180-foot long pier used by tour and commercial vessels with approximately 60 feet of space on the south side of the dock (east end) available for use by the public. The park beachfront offers a landing area for canoes and kayaks. The boat ramp just to the north of the public dock requires an access card from April through October.

RESTAURANTS
Coffee & Dessert (6)
Casual (21)
Fine Dining (10)
Fast Food (7)

KIRKLAND MARINA PARK	
Area	East shore of Lake Washington
Address	25 Lake Shore Plaza, Kirkland
Hours	All Hours
Length of Stay	72 Hours (self-pay overnight)
Tie Up Space	66 medium height slips and approximately 200 feet of dock space
Suitable For	Yachts, Cruiser, Runabouts, Canoes
Type	Public, City of Kirkland
Contact	(425) 587-3340 www.ci.kirkland.wa.us
Fuel	None
Launch	One lane (pre-purchased access card required April – October available from City of Kirkland)
Insider Tips	❑ Check the events calendar at www.ci.kirkland.wa.us as the extensive dock can fill during events at park or in the city. ❑ Have extra lines and fenders as the water can be rough on busy days.

Kirkland offers a wide variety of restaurants from which to choose, ranging from fine dining and casual sit-down, to fast foods and coffee & dessert shops. The restaurants listed in this section are all within easy walking distance from the Kirkland public dock.

Another option for some quick eats and unique shopping is the "Farmers Market" held every Wednesday from noon to 7 p.m. May 1st – October 16th in the 200 block of Park Lane.

If you happen to be in Kirkland on an especially busy day and don't mind some extra walking, there are some fine restaurants further east of the downtown core towards the freeway; follow Central Way east until you come to Kirkland Park Place.

KIRKLAND
Marina Park

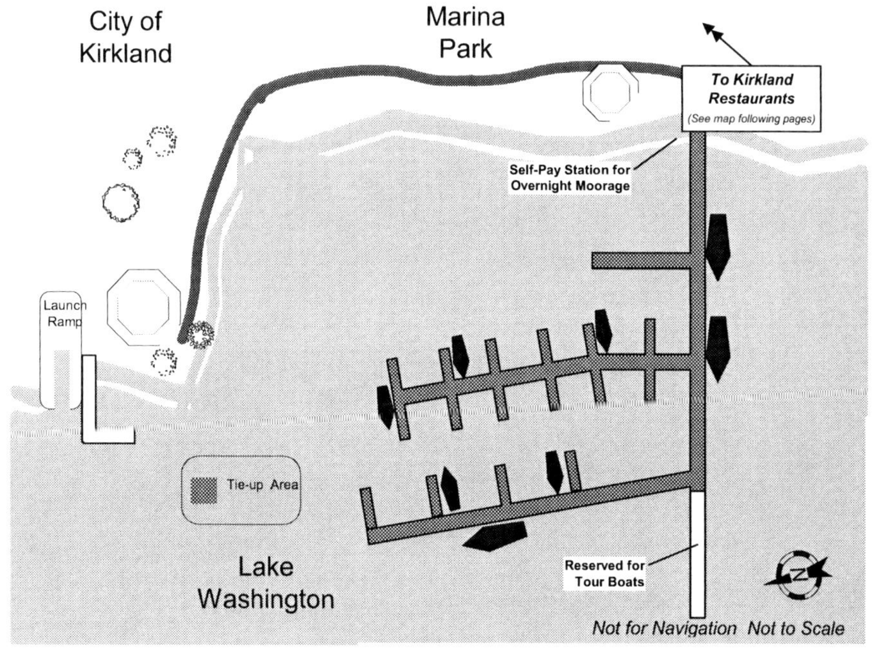

City of Kirkland
Marina Park
To Kirkland Restaurants
(See map following pages)
Self-Pay Station for Overnight Moorage
Launch Ramp
Tie-up Area
Lake Washington
Reserved for Tour Boats
Not for Navigation Not to Scale

KIRKLAND
Marina Park

CASUAL DINING RESTAURANTS			
Cactus	Tacos, Ensaladas	121 Park Lane	(425) 893-9799 www.cactusrestaurants.com
Coyote Creek Pizza	Pizza, Salad, Pasta	228 Central Way	(425) 822-2226 www.coyotecreekpizza.com
George's Place	Burgers, Pasta, Greek	108 Kirkland Ave.	(425) 827-6622
Hanuman Thai Café	Thai Cuisine	115 Central Way	(425) 605-2181
Hector's	Fish, Pasta, Steak	112 Lake Street	(425) 827-4811
Jalisco Mexican	Burritos, Tostados	115 Park Lane	(425) 822-3355
Kirkland Ave Pub	Beer, Pizza	205B Kirkland Ave.	(425) 576-9032
Lakeshore Veggie	Vegetarian Cuisine	15 Lake St. #103	(425) 889-2850
Marina Cantina	Shellfish, Tostados, Tacos	105 Lake Street S.	(425) 576-5600 www.marinacantina.com
Marina Park Grill	Fish, Shellfish, Brunch	89 Kirkland Ave.	(425) 889-9000 www.marinaparkgrill.com
Papa Johns	Pizza	211 Third Street	(425) 803-8000
Pasta Ya Gotcha	Pastas & Salads	123 Lake Street	(425) 889-1511 www.pastayagotcha.com
Sake House	Sushi & Grill	166 Lake Street S.	(425) 822-8245 www.sakehousekirkland.com
Santorini Greek Grill	Mouska, Salads	106 Central Way	(425) 822-0555
Sasi's Café	Sandwiches, Soups	130 Lake Street S.	(425) 889-2411
The Slip	Burgers, Fish Burger	80 Kirkland Ave.	(425) 739-0033
Thin Pan Siam Bistro	Thai Cuisine	170 Lake Street	(425) 827-4000
Triple J Café	Soups, Sandwiches	101 Central Way	(425) 822-7319
Wilde Rover	Irish Pub	111 Central Way	(425) 822-8940
Wing Dome	Chicken, Salads, Sandwiches	232 Central Way	(425) 822-9464 www.wingdome.com
Zeek's Pizza	Pizzas, Salads	124 Park Lane	(425) 893-8646

FINE DINING RESTAURANTS			
Anthony's HomePort	Fish, Shellfish, Brunch	135 Lake Street S.	(425) 822-0225 www.anthonys.com
Calabria Ristorante Italiano	Pasta, Pizza, Veal	132 Lake Street S.	(425) 822-7350 calabriaitalianrestaurant.com
Fish Cafe	Fish, Shellfish, Lamb, Brunch	205 Lake Street S.	(425) 822-3553 www.fishcafe.com
Lai-Thai	Thai Cuisine	120B Park Lane	(425) 739-9747
Lynn's Bistro	Duck, Fish, Lamb	214 Central Way	(425) 889-2808
Mixtura	Andean Cuisine	148 Lake Street S.	(425) 803-3310
Raga	Cuisine of India	212 Central Way	(425) 827-3300 www.ragarestaurant.com
Ristorante Paradiso	Pastas, Fish	120A Park Lane	(425) 889-8601 www.ristoranteparadiso.com
Sentesa	Asian Cuisine	107 Lake Street	(425) 822-9082
21 Club	Steak, Lobster	21 Central Way	(425) 822-1515 www.21central.com

FAST FOOD RESTAURANTS			
Café Happy Asian	Vegetables	102 Kirkland Ave.	(425) 822-9696
I Luv Teriyaki	Chicken, Pork	104 Kirkland Ave.	(425) 739-8899
Subway	Deli Sandwiches	255 Central Way	(425) 889-0711 www.subway.com
Taco Del Mar	Tacos, Burritos	210 Main Street	(425) 827-0177 www.tacodelmar.com
Tiki Joe's Wet Bar	Beer, Burgers	106 Kirkland Ave.	(425) 827-8300
Tokyo Grill Teriyaki	Chicken, Pork	238 Park Lane	(425) 822-3473
World Wrapps	Tortilla wrapped Sandwiches	124 Lake Street S.	(425) 827-9727 www.worldwrapps.com

KIRKLAND
Marina Park

COFFEE & DESSERT			
Ben & Jerry's	Ice cream, Yogurt	176 Lake Street S.	(425) 576-1609 www.benjerrys.com
Coffee & Cone	Coffee, Ice cream	1 Lake Shore Plaza	(425) 827-7098
Kahili Coffee	Espresso, Pastries	105 Lake Street S.	(425) 576-5600
Market Street Perk	Coffee, Pastries	631 Market Street	(425) 828-7564
Reality Coffee	Coffee, Pastries	116 Lake Street	(425) 827-0890
Tully's Coffee	Coffee, Pastries	164 Lake Street S.	(425) 803-0344 www.tullys.com

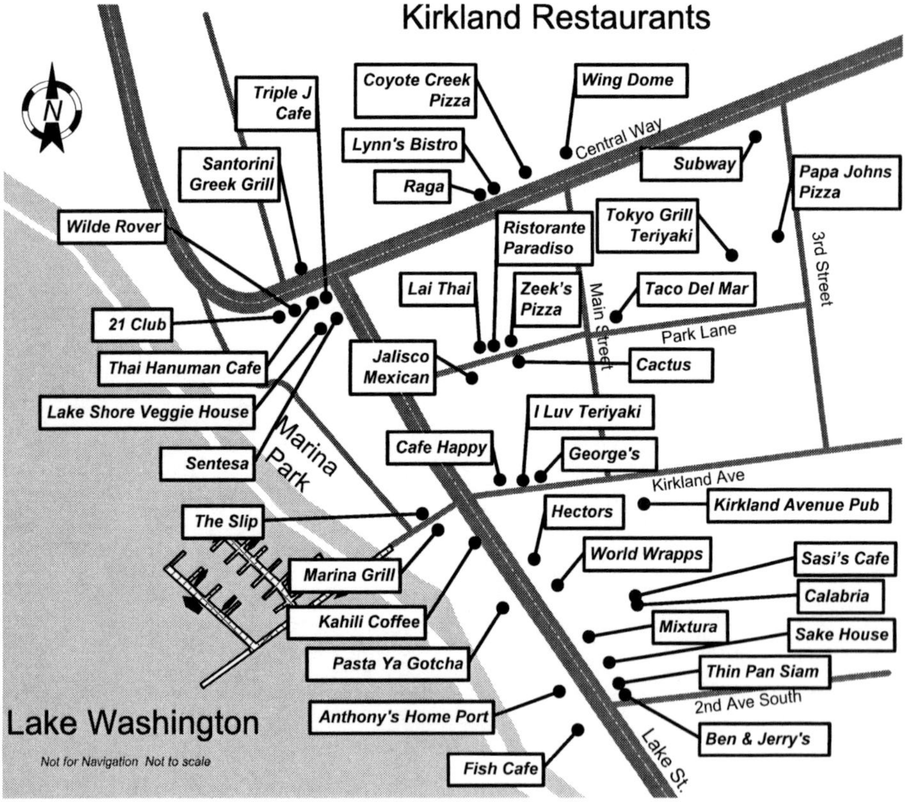

Marina Park

KIRKLAND

Second Street Dock

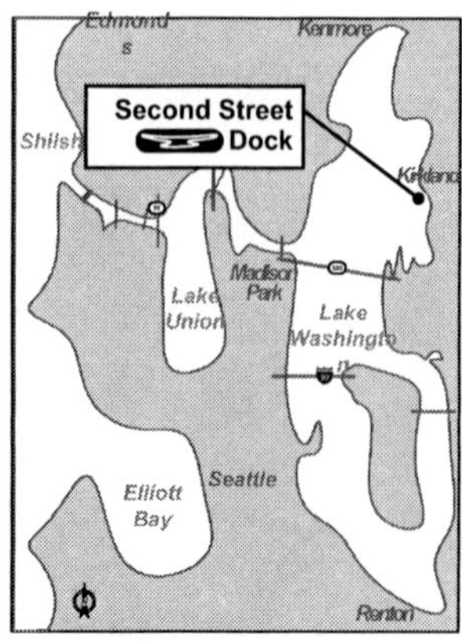

The Second Street Dock is located south of the Kirkland Marina Park public docks and south and adjacent to the Kirkland Yacht Club Marina docks. This City of Kirkland street-end dock is available to boaters for day stays at no charge. Guest tie-up space is only on the south side of the Second Street Dock.

Located between Anthony's HomePort restaurant and the Fish Café, the Second Street Dock is a convenient tie-up space for either restaurant. Central downtown Kirkland restaurants are within easy walking distance of the Second Street Dock, making this location a good alternative if the Kirkland Marina Park docks are full.

RESTAURANTS
Anthony's HomePort
Fish Cafe

SECOND STREET DOCK	
Area	East shore of Lake Washington
Address	200 Lake Street South, Kirkland
Hours	No Overnight Moorage
Length of Stay	8 hours
Tie Up Space	400' of medium height fixed dock
Suitable For	Yachts, Cruisers, Runabouts
Type	Public, Kirkland Parks Dept.
Contact	(425) 587-3340
Insider Tips	❑ Tie on south side of dock only

KIRKLAND
Second Street Dock

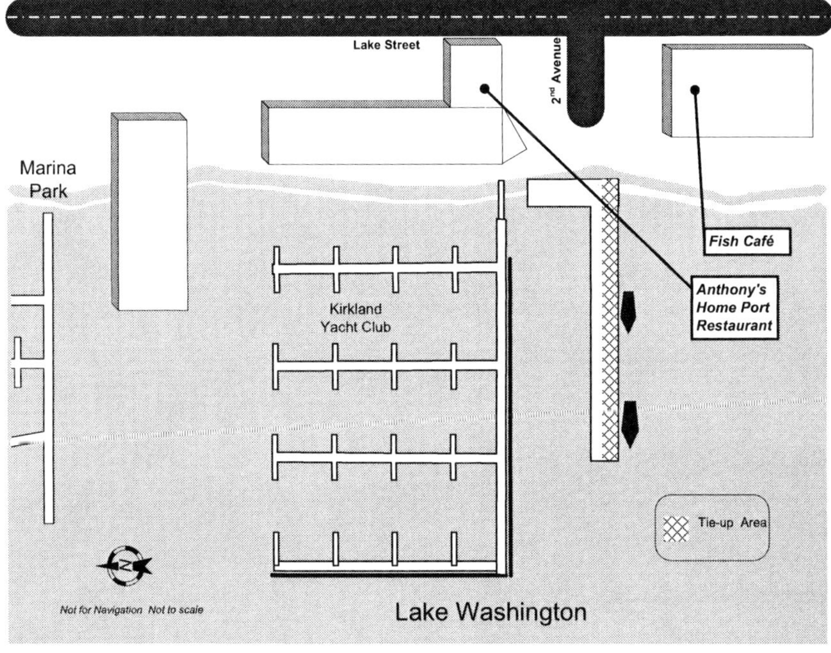

KIRKLAND
Second Street Dock

ANTHONY'S HOMEPORT

Anthony's in Kirkland opened in 1975 and was the very first Anthony's Homeport, which specializes in fresh Northwest seafood featuring oven roasted Halibut, Alder planked salmon, Dungeness Crab, half shell oysters, Yellowfin Ahi, and many more tasty seafood dishes. Anthony's owns and operates their own seafood company for the purpose of supplying their guests with fresh premium fish and shellfish. A tradition at Anthony's Home Port for 28 years is the "all you can eat Dungeness crab feed" served Sunday evenings. Anthony's offers seating with views of Lake Washington and the Kirkland Yacht Club. Outdoor summer seating is available on the south side with views of the Olympics and the Seattle skyline.

Hours	Brunch: 10am - 2pm Sundays Dinner: 5pm - 9:30pm Mon-Thur 5pm - 10:30pm Fri & Sat 3pm - 9:30pm Sundays
Serving	Brunch, Dinner
Price	$ 8-$16 Brunch $16-$30 Dinner
Reservations	Recommended
Environment	Business Casual / Dressy
Outdoor Seating	Yes, Summer Months
Contact Info.	(425) 822-0225 www.anthonysrestaurants.com
Notables	❑ Sunday Crab Feed

Help other boaters
with their lines.

KIRKLAND
Second Street Dock

FISH CAFE

The Fish Café is located on the third floor of the Chaffey Building at 205 Lake Street next to the Second Street Dock. The Café has dark warm woods, large picture windows, and a combination of tables and booths in a tiered fashion to take advantage of the beautiful views of the Seattle skyline, the Olympic Mountains, and the Kirkland Yacht Club Marina. Fresh fish is the entrée focus with additional offerings of steak, lamb, and chicken. Try the Seared Rare Ahi Tuna with black pepper fingerling potatoes, red onion jam, and toasted shallot oil or try the Seared Alaskan Sea Scallops in a vegetable ragout and porcini broth. Delicious desserts and dessert wines provide the finishing touch. The Separate bar is an ideal place to enjoy good appetizers or desserts during the special happy hour.

Hours	Dinner: 5pm – 9:30pm Daily Closing Hours Vary Happy Hour: 4pm – 6pm 9pm – Closing
Serving	Dinner
Price	$26 - $40
Reservations	Recommended
Environment	Business Casual / Dressy
Outdoor Seating	No
Contact Info.	(425) 822-3553 www.fishcafe.com
Notables	❑ Fish Café Newsletter

KIRKLAND
Settlers Landing

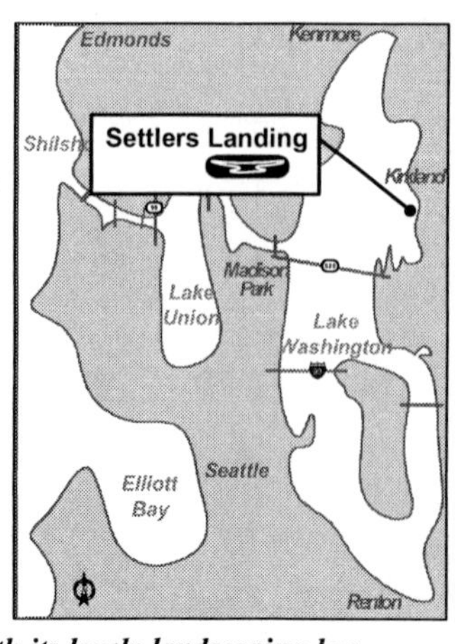

"Settlers Landing" tucked between private docks on the shores of Kirkland is a hidden gem and often missed by boaters. This street-end public dock has plenty of tie-up space on the north side of the dock. The south side of the dock is for private moorage only. Although the sign for the public indicates a maximum stay of 30 minutes, the City of Kirkland has told us that longer stays while dining at the Lakeside Café would be appropriate if needed. Day-long or extended stays are not permitted.

RESTAURANT	
	Lakeside Cafe

The Lakeside Cafe is just across the street from Settlers Landing and is a pleasant location for a casual breakfast or an afternoon meal. The small park with its lovely landscaping has an attractive pathway leading up to Lake Street.

SETTLERS LANDING		
	Area	East Shore of Lake Washington (South of downtown Kirkland)
	Address	1006 Lake Street South
	Hours	Restaurant Hours
	Length of Stay	30 Minutes
	Tie Up Space	Approx. 80 Feet
	Suitable For	Cruisers, Runabouts
	Type	Public, City of Kirkland
	Contact	(425) 828-1213 (425) 828-7954

KIRKLAND
Settlers Landing

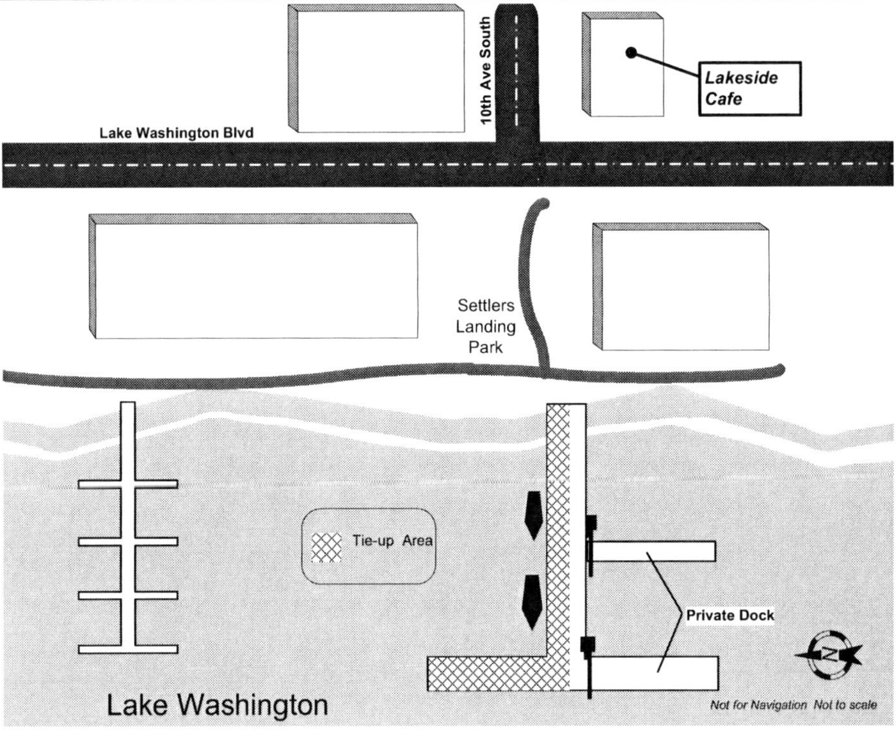

10th Ave South

Lakeside Cafe

Lake Washington Blvd

Settlers Landing Park

Tie-up Area

Private Dock

Lake Washington

N

Not for Navigation Not to scale

KIRKLAND
Settlers Landing

THE LAKESIDE CAFE

The Lakeside Café is located directly across the street from the Settlers Landing public dock at 1006 Lake Street. The Café offers cold sandwiches, hot sandwiches, charbroiled beef and chicken burgers, salads, soft drinks, and an espresso bar. Café favorites include the egg salad sandwich, the mushroom burger, and the hot smoked turkey sandwich. To-go box-lunches are also available. A special treat at The Lakeside Café is breakfast on Saturday mornings from 9 am until noon. The breakfast menu includes omelets, breakfast sandwiches, French Toast, pancakes, home-style potatoes, and combos with bacon, sausage, and ham. Seating is available on the outdoor patio during the summer months with filtered views of Lake Washington.

Hours	Breakfast: 9am – Noon Saturdays Lunch/Dinner: 11am – 3pm Mon-Sat And 5:30pm – 8pm
Serving	Lunch Dinner
Price	\$4 - \$8
Reservations	No
Cuisine	Burgers, Sandwiches
Environment	Casual
Outdoor Seating	Yes, Patio, Summer Months
Contact Info.	(425) 822-5583

Settlers Landing

LESCHI

Leschi Landing

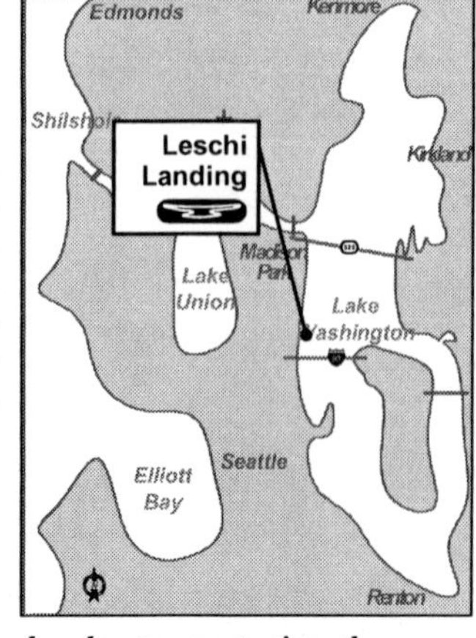

Leschi offers stunning views of the Bellevue skyline with a selection of four restaurant venues and one coffee shop. The park was the campsite of chief Leschi, who was executed by Governor Isaac Stevens for participation in an attack on the settlement in 1856. In 1889 this site became an amusement park at the end of the Cable Railway's trolley line and housed the town's first zoo, gardens, and a casino. Locals rode the lake steamer east to Mercer Island as well as the cable cars west to Yesler Street.

Leschi is located on the western shore of Lake Washington midway between the two floating bridges and its public dock can be used by those dining at any of the eateries in the Leschi area. There is adequate tie-up space with a breakwater protecting the Leschi marina; however, the transient tie-up area is vulnerable to heavy wave action from "Wake Washington".

The BluWater Bistro, Daniel's Broiler, Pert's Deli, the Ruby Asian, and Starbucks are all within easy walking distance from the Leschi public dock.

RESTAURANTS
BluWater Bistro
Daniels Broiler
Pert's Deli
Ruby Asian
Starbucks Coffee

LESCHI LANDING	
Area	West Shore Lake Washington
Address	102 Lakeside Avenue Seattle
Hours	All Hours
Length of Stay	2 hours
Tie Up Space	200 feet of medium high dock
Suitable For	Cruisers, Runabouts, Canoes
Type	Public
Contact	(206) 684-4075
Fuel	None
Launch	None
Insider Tips	❑ Use plenty of fenders to protect against the rather high dock and wave action.

LESCHI
Leschi Landing

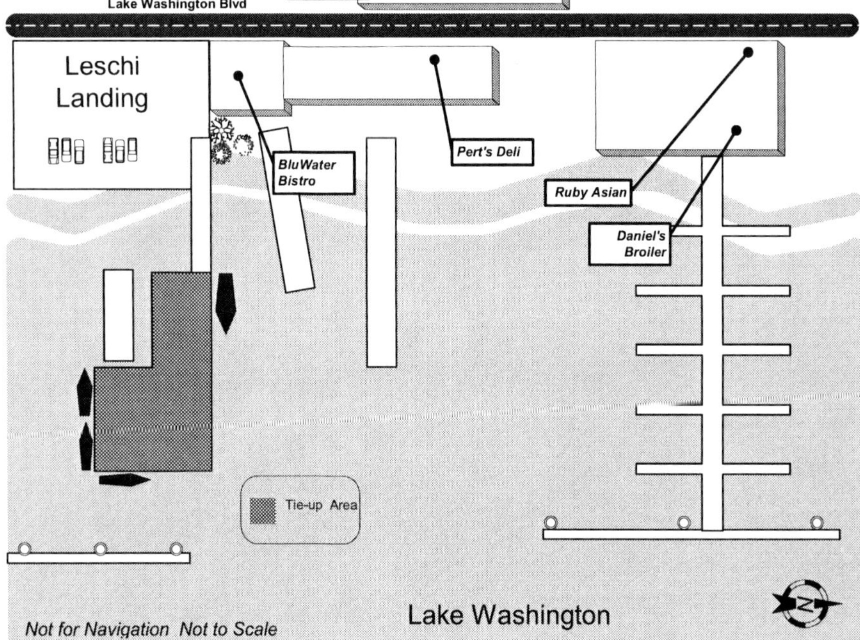

LESCHI
Leschi Landing

BLUWATER BISTRO

The latest BluWater Bistro is located in what use to be the Leschi Café; and after some innovative remodeling, the newest BluWater has quickly become a popular destination. The restaurant has a new open floor plan with a cozy fireplace in the center surrounded by conversational couches. The new seating arrangement for dining varies from intimate tables for two up to large round tables for group settings. The new bar area has folding windows that open out to the summer patio seating area from which diners can look through the restaurant on out to the water. The good use of space has brought everyone together in an open friendly atmosphere. The same tasty and creative menu items are available here like those at the Lake Union BluWater location. For dinner, try the almond crusted Alaskan Halibut served with a spicy vegetable ragout and baby red potatoes, or try the roasted stuffed pork chop with herb-pecan dressing served with a baked stuffed apple and garlic mashed potatoes. For a great breakfast meal, try the spinach & goat cheese omelet.

Hours	Breakfast/Lunch 9am – 4pm Sat & Sun Dinner: 4pm – 1am Daily
Serving	Breakfast, Dinner
Price	$7 - $19
Reservations	Recommended
Environment	Casual / Business Casual
Outdoor Seating	Yes, Patio, Summer Months
Contact Info.	(206) 328-2233
Notables	❑ Lunch Sat & Sun Only ❑ Koby's Take-Out window - Summers

PERT'S A DELI ON LESCHI

Pert's, a Deli on Leschi, is a great option for some good quick eats offering soups, sandwiches, bagels, rolls, breads, and a nice selection of pasta salads. For a warm up, enjoy a good cup of espresso along with their selection of cookies, brownies, and coffee cakes. Breakfast includes filled croissants, scones, cinnamon rolls, and a variety of omelets, served until noon on Saturdays and Sundays.

Hours	Breakfast/Lunch: 7am – 5pm Daily Full Breakfast: 8:30am – Noon Sat & Sun
Serving	Breakfast, Lunch
Price	$5-$10
Reservations	No
Environment	Casual
Outdoor Seating	Yes, Sidewalk, Summer Months
Contact Info.	(206) 325-0277
Notables	❑ Call ahead orders to go

DANIELS BROILER

Daniels Broiler at Leschi is housed in a renovated Boat House and this historic building has been appointed with warm woods and beautiful chandeliers. The Leschi location serves the same delicious seasoned and seared USDA prime grade steaks offered at all Daniel Broilers; the Filet Mignon, Rib-Eye, Porterhouse, Top Sirloin, and New York steaks. Fresh seafood, chicken, lamb, and veal are also available. Daniels serves award winning wines, and every Sunday night is "Prime Wine Night" with great wines at half price. Daniels at Leschi has the distinction of beautiful views of Mount Rainier, the Cascades, and the Bellevue skyline, which is especially stunning at sunset.

Hours	Dinner: 5pm - 10pm Sun-Thurs 5pm - 11pm Fri & Sat Happy Hour: 4:30pm – 6:30pm Daily
Serving	Dinner
Price	$19-$40
Reservations	Recommended
Environment	Business Casual / Dressy
Outdoor Seating	Yes, Deck, Summer Months
Contact Info.	(206) 329-4191 www.swartzbrothersrestaurants.com
Notables	❑ Neighborhood Wine Night (Sun.) ❑ Happy Hour 4:30-6:30 pm daily in the Lounge only (special price) ❑ Piano Bar Thur-Sat ❑ On-line Reservations

RUBY ASIAN

The Ruby Asian serves an extensive Asian menu, including Thai cuisine and dishes from China and Japan. Little chili peppers marked next to the menu selections indicate if dishes are mild, hot, med. hot, very hot, or extremely hot. Many of the chicken, beef, and shrimp Thai dishes are served with tofu and various spicy sauces. Japanese dishes like teriyaki and yakisoba are mild menu items as well as many of the Asian chicken, beef, pork, and seafood selections. The restaurant is comfortable and attractive with fan-folded napkins on the tables, Asian art work adorning the walls, and soothing listening music playing in the background.

Hours	Lunch/Dinner: 11am – 9:30pm Mon-Thur 11am – 10pm Fridays Noon – 9:30pm Saturdays 3pm – 9:30pm Sundays Winter Hours Vary
Serving	Lunch, Dinner
Price	$6 - $13
Reservations	Recommended
Environment	Casual / Business Casual
Outdoor Seating	No
Contact Info.	(206) 322-7288
Notables	❑ Spicy Thai Food Available

MADISON PARK

Madison Park Landing

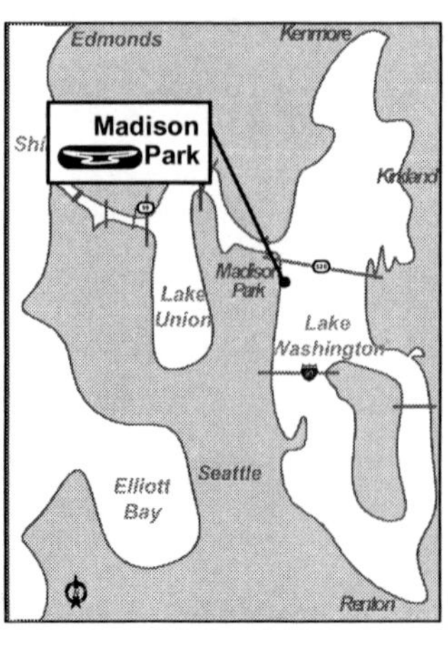

One of the best destinations on Lake Washington for hungry boaters, the Madison Park Community preserves its old town 1920's charm of small shops and eateries. Summers are especially fun with a number of outdoor café tables creating an old European charm.

Boaters may tie up for 2 hours at the Madison Park Dock located just south of the 520 floating bridge on the west end. Look for the tall imposing apartment buildings; the Madison Park and Dock is just to the north. The dock is quite high and is best suited for yachts. Runabouts and cruisers should use an anchor line off the bow (facing east) in addition to bow and stern tie to the dock.

RESTAURANTS	
	Coffee & Dessert (4)
	Fine Dining (2)
	Casual Dining (8)

After enjoying the delightful shops and eateries, don't miss the Pioneer Museum, which is open the second Sunday of each month from 1 pm to 4 pm located at 1642 – 43rd Ave. East.

MADISON PARK LANDING		
	Area	West central Lake Washington South of 520 Bridge
	Address	East Madison & 43rd Ave East, Seattle
	Hours	No Overnight Moorage
	Length of Stay	2 hours
	Tie Up Space	60 feet of high fixed dock
	Suitable For	Yachts, Cruisers
	Type	Public, City of Seattle Parks Dept.
	Contact	(206) 684-4075
	Fuel	None
	Launch	None
	Insider Tips	❑ High dock can be difficult tie for boats with low freeboard ❑ Runabouts should use an additional anchor line off the bow. ❑ Exposed tie-up area with no breakwater. Use lots of fenders, securely tie with spring lines

In 1890, Madison Park was an amusement center with carnival rides and was also the location of Seattle's first baseball field. The park included an ornate boathouse, piers, and a wooden promenade. The "Mosquito Fleet" boats made regular stops at Madison Park. The park area was set aside for public use by Judge John McGilvra, who had purchased 420 acres of land. To reach his land, he cut a straight-line road in 1864 through the forest from downtown Seattle to Madison Park; and Madison Street today is the only direct route in Seattle between salt water and fresh water. John McGilvra also began a cable car route, which ran every two minutes in the summers.

MADISON PARK
Madison Park Landing

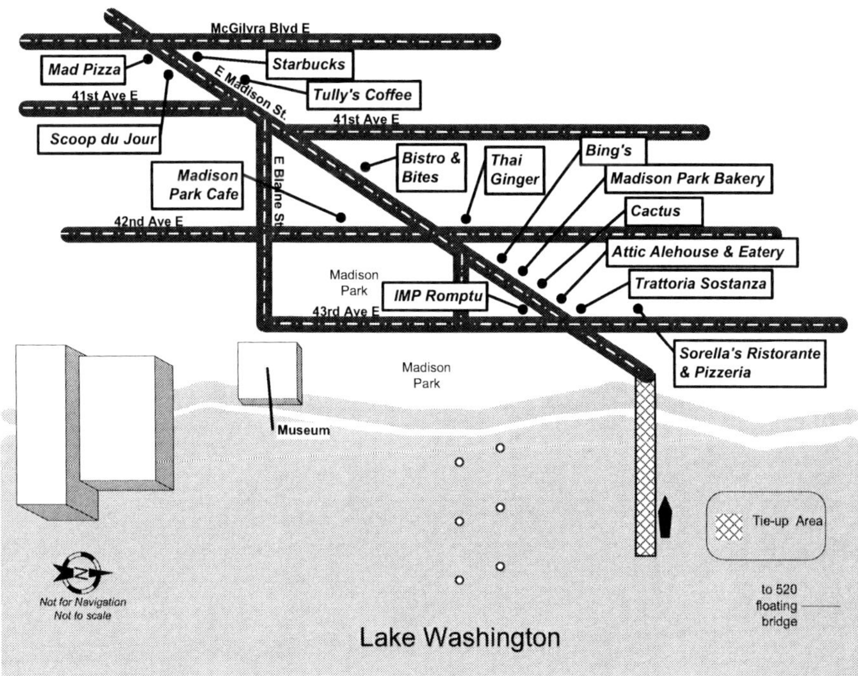
McGilvra Blvd E
Mad Pizza
Starbucks
E Madison St.
Tully's Coffee
41st Ave E
41st Ave E
Scoop du Jour
Bistro & Bites
Thai Ginger
Bing's
Madison Park Cafe
E Blaine St
Madison Park Bakery
Cactus
42nd Ave E
Attic Alehouse & Eatery
Madison Park
IMP Romptu
Trattoria Sostanza
43rd Ave E
Sorella's Ristorante & Pizzeria
Madison Park
Museum
Tie-up Area
Not for Navigation
Not to scale
to 520 floating bridge
Lake Washington

MADISON PARK
Madison Park Landing

COFFEE & DESSERTS			
Madison Park Bakery	Cakes, Cookies, Pies, Pastries	4214 E. Madison St.	(206) 322-3238
Scoop du Jour Ice Creamery	Ice Cream,	4029 E. Madison St.	(206) 325-9562
Starbucks Coffee	Coffee, Pastries	4000 E. Madison St.	(206) 329-3736
Tully's Coffee	Coffee, Pastries	4036 E. Madison St.	(206) 329-6659

FINE DINING RESTAURANTS			
IMP Romptu	Steaks, Chicken, Salmon	4235 E. Madison St.	(206) 860-1569
Trattoria Sostanza	Pastas, Seafood, Pork, Veal, Chicken, Veg.	1927 – 43rd Ave. E.	(206) 324-9701

CASUAL DINING RESTAURANTS			
Attic Alehouse & Eatery	Burgers, Sandwiches, Salads, Pastas	4226 E. Madison St.	(206) 323-3131
Bing's	Burgers, Chicken, BBQ	4200 E. Madison	(206) 323-8623
Bistro & Bites	Deli Meals, Sandwiches	4122 E. Madison	(206) 328-2492
Cactus	Tacos, Ensaladas	4220 E. Madison St.	(206) 324-4140
Mad Pizza	Pizzas, Salads	4021 E. Madison St.	(206) 329-7037
Madison Park Café	Omelets, Pancakes, Pasta, Fish, Lamb, Steak	1807 – 42nd Ave. E.	(206) 324-2626
Sorella's Ristorante & Pizzeria	Pasta, Pizza, Sandwiches	4234 E. Madison St.	(206) 323-1393
Thai Ginger	Soups, Noodles, Seafood, Chicken	1841 – 42nd Ave. E.	(206) 324-6467

MADISON PARK

Madison Park Landing

RENTON
Coulon Park

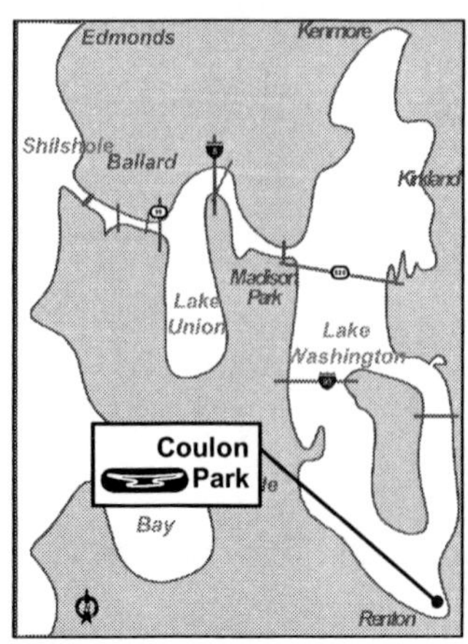

The Gene Coulon Memorial Park, a Renton City park, is located on the south end of Lake Washington. This land was once an old ship storage facility. Gene Coulon, Director for 30 years of Renton Parks & Recreation, was instrumental in acquiring the first tract of land for this beautiful park. The exceptionally designed park provides covered outdoor picnic areas, gazebos, and boardwalks with intimate tables and benches on floats. Stretch your legs on the shore walks and jogging trails, which run north and south along the Nature Island Sanctuary. Off the swimming beach, are tennis courts and a playground. The park is open to the public from 7 am to dusk year-round.

RESTAURANTS
Ivar's
Kidd Valley

Boaters can choose from two fast-food eateries, Ivar's and Kidd Valley, both located immediately in front of the tie-up areas.

The harbor basin at Coulon has 12 floating dock slips for boats up to 25 feet with additional space for larger boats along the inside east wall, a medium high fixed dock. Boat stays are limited to 4 hours. The four-lane boat launch is immediately south of the tie-up areas.

The many amenities of Coulon Park make this location a popular year-round destination. There may be a wait for space during the summer months.

When heading north from Coulon Park, take note of this unique location, where you can see the Bellevue city skyline and the Seattle city skyline from the same vantage point with Mercer Island nestled between the two cities.

COULON PARK	
Area	South End of Lake Washington
Address	1201 Lake Washington Blvd. N. Renton, Washington
Hours	7:00am to Dusk
Length of Stay	4 hours
Tie Up Space	Medium high dock Floating dock slips
Suitable For	Yachts, Cruisers, Runabouts, Canoes
Type	Public, City of Renton Parks Dept.
Contact	(425) 430-6712
Fuel	None
Launch	4 Ramps, 2 Lanes Each
Insider Tips	❑ Three reservable picnic shelters ❑ Interpretive botanical walk

RENTON
Coulon Park

MOORAGE FOR
ON SHORE
ACTIVITIES
4 HOUR LIMIT
SLOW
NO
WAKE

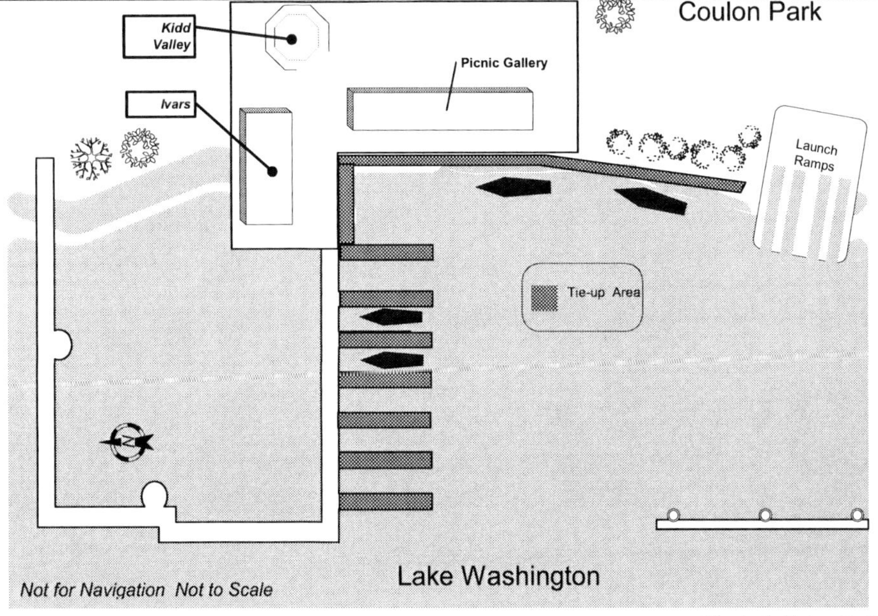
Coulon Park
Kidd Valley
Ivars
Picnic Gallery
Launch Ramps
Tie-up Area
Lake Washington
Not for Navigation Not to Scale

RENTON
Coulon Park

IVAR'S SEAFOOD BAR

Ivar's Seafood Bars provide the same quality and history that the founder, Ivar Haglund began in 1938. Fish-'n-chips and the original clam chowder continue to be favorite Pacific Northwest treats enjoyed by many at this park with commanding views of Lake Washington and the Olympic Mountains.

Hours	Lunch/Dinner: 10:30am - 8pm Daily Open till 9pm summer months
Serving	Lunch, Dinner
Price	$5-$16
Reservations	No
Cuisine	Seafood, Fast Foods
Environment	Casual
Outdoor Seating	Yes, Park Seating
Contact Info.	(425) 226-2122

KIDD VALLEY

Kidd Valley's made-to-order burgers and hand-mixed shakes can be traced back to its founder John Morris, who had a fondness for tasty burgers and shakes. Morris sold his Kidd Valley restaurants to Ivar's in 1989. Kidd Valley burgers are made from fresh hamburger rather than frozen patties and the onion rings are made with fresh Walla Walla Onions in season.

Hours	10:30am - 8pm Daily Open till 9pm during summer months
Serving	Lunch, Dinner
Price	$3-$5
Reservations	No
Cuisine	Hamburgers, Shakes, Fast Foods
Environment	Casual
Outdoor Seating	Yes, Park Seating
Contact Info.	(425) 277-3324

Coulon Park

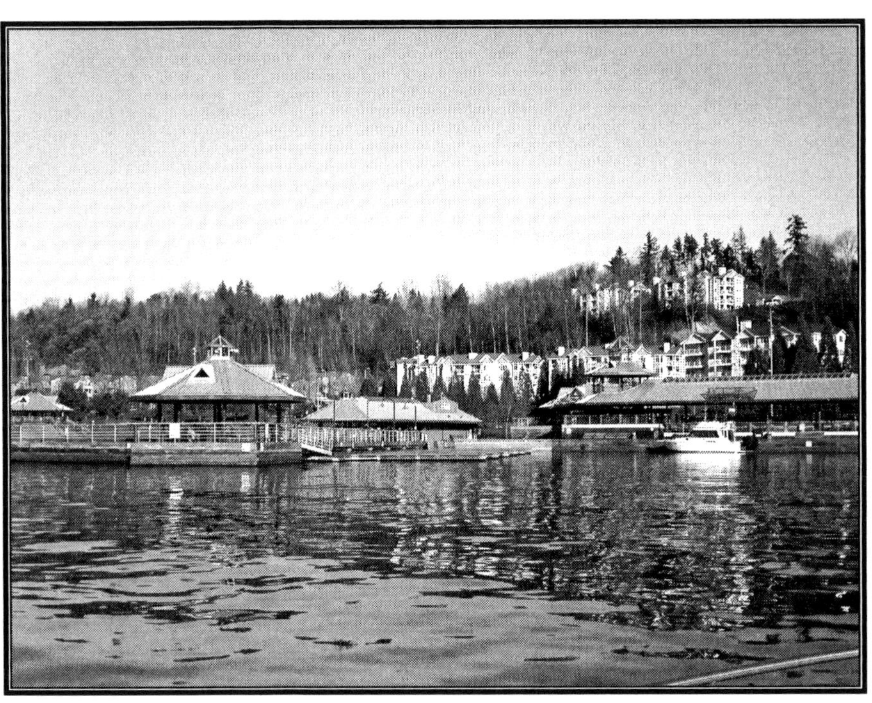

Lake water levels vary seasonally by up to 2 feet; highest in Spring, lowest early Fall.

Portage Bay & North Lake Union

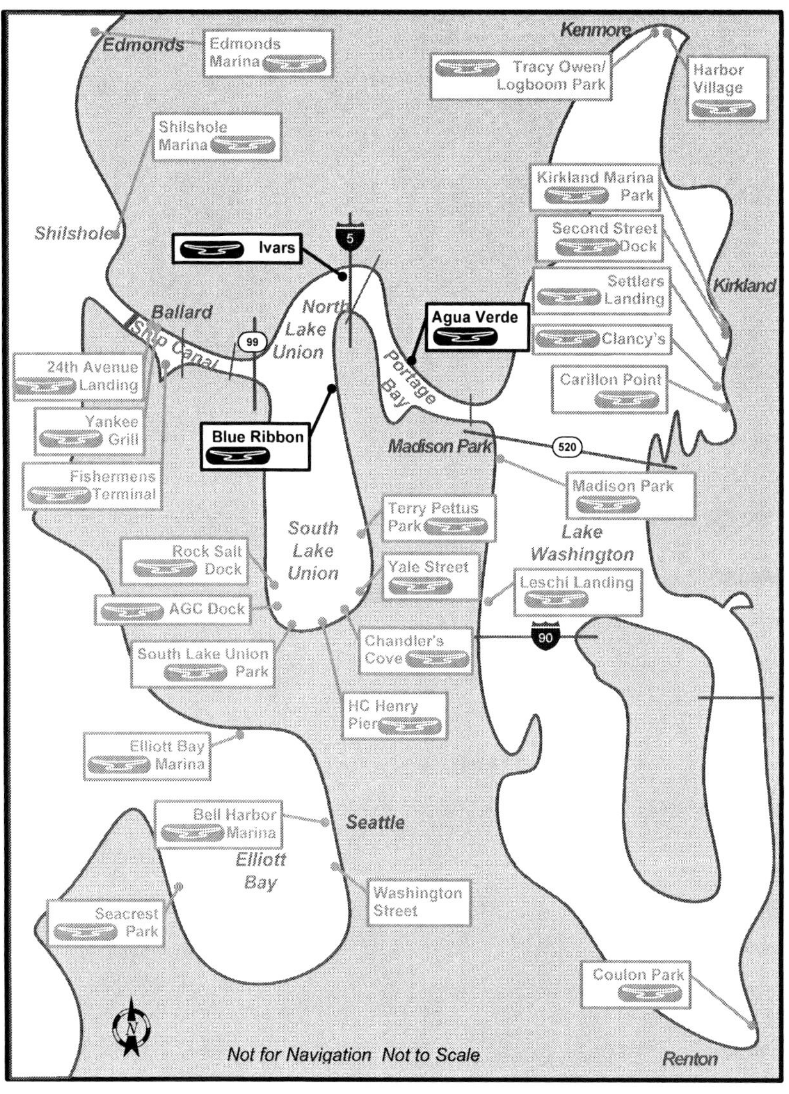

Kenmore
Edmonds
Edmonds Marina
Tracy Owen/ Logboom Park
Harbor Village
Shilshole Marina
Kirkland Marina Park
Second Street Dock
Shilshole
Ivars
5
Settlers Landing
Kirkland
Ballard
North Lake Union
Agua Verde
Ship Canal
99
Clancy's
24th Avenue Landing
Portage Bay
Carillon Point
Yankee Grill
Blue Ribbon
Madison Park
520
Fishermens Terminal
Madison Park
Terry Pettus Park
South Lake Union
Lake Washington
Rock Salt Dock
Yale Street
Leschi Landing
AGC Dock
Chandler's Cove
90
South Lake Union Park
HC Henry Pier
Elliott Bay Marina
Bell Harbor Marina
Seattle
Elliott Bay
Washington Street
Seacrest Park
Coulon Park
Not for Navigation Not to Scale
Renton

PORTAGE BAY

Agua Verde Guest Dock

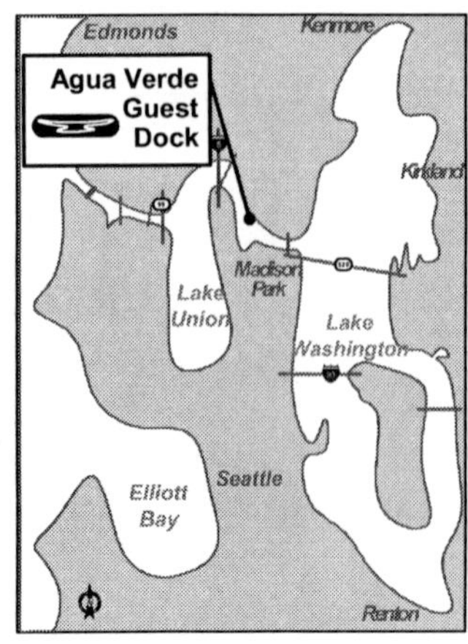

Sporting a paddle rental in the lower half of the building, the Agua Verde restaurant landing is best suited for runabouts and smaller watercraft.

A limited amount of guest space is available to boaters while dining at the Agua Verde. The tie-up space is immediately in front of the restaurant building on the east side of the floating dock with approximately 40 feet of space.

RESTAURANT	Agua Verde

This is not the destination for the faint of heart; the channel is narrow and shallow and the guest space is not well marked. Once you have succeeded with your tie-up, you will be rewarded with excellent food at Agua Verde.

AGUA VERDE GUEST DOCK		
	Area	Northwest side of Portage Bay
	Address	1303 NE Boat St., Seattle
	Length of Stay	While Dining
	Tie Up Space	Approximately 40 Feet
	Suitable For	Runabouts, Canoes
	Type	Private, Agua Verde Cafe
	Contact	(206) 545-8570
	Insider Tips	❑ Limited tie-up space ❑ Please be considerate of private moorage ❑ Shallow water with lots of milfoil and sea grasses

PORTAGE BAY
Agua Verde Guest Dock

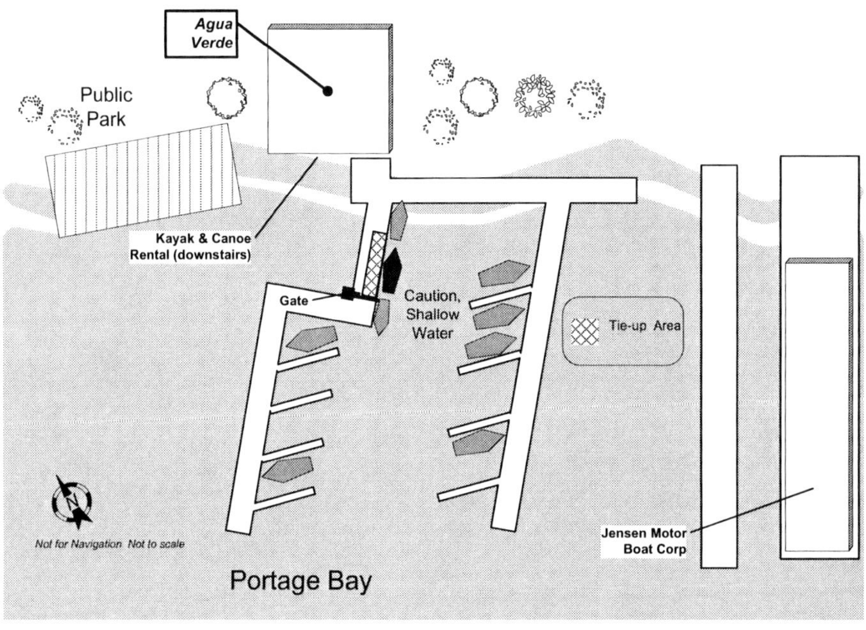

PORTAGE BAY

Agua Verde Guest Dock

AGUA VERDE CAFÉ

The Agua Verde is a hidden gem in Portage Bay not always noticed by boaters. Located in a renovated house with brightly colored walls and a festive décor, the Agua Verde creates only authentic natural Mexican recipes. The Tacos de la Casa is the signature item at Agua Verde and a variety is available all day. Try the Taco De mero with grilled Halibut, cabbage, and creamy avocado sauce or the De bagre with spicy catfish, lettuce, salsa mexicana, and creamy avocado sauce. During lunch, the food is served cafeteria style. (There is also a take-out window, which is open Mon-Fri.) The dinner menu includes a different special each night. Monday is Pollo en mole with dark chicken meat in a Oaxaca sauce made with dried chiles, Mexican chocolate, fruits and spices. The Margaritas and house-made soft drinks are especially good. Mexican beers and wine are also available. For dessert try the Mexican chocolate cake with prickly pear syrup. From the Café and summer deck, you can view the activity of the Agua Verde Paddle Club located downstairs and enjoy the vista over Portage Bay with its many houseboats.

Hours	Lunch: 11am - 4pm Mon-Sat Dinner: 5pm - 9pm Mon-Sat Happy Hour: 4pm – 6pm Mon-Sat
Serving	Lunch, Dinner
Price	$5-$7 Lunch $8-10 Dinner
Reservations	Yes, Groups of 8 or more
Environment	Casual
Cuisine	Authentic Mexican
Outdoor Seating	Yes, Restaurant Deck, Summers Tables at Adjacent Park
Contact Info.	(206) 545-8570 www.aguaverde.com
Notables	❑ Live music Mondays ❑ To-Go orders ❑ Private groups on Sundays

PORTAGE BAY

Agua Verde Guest Dock

NORTH LAKE UNION

Blue Ribbon Guest Dock

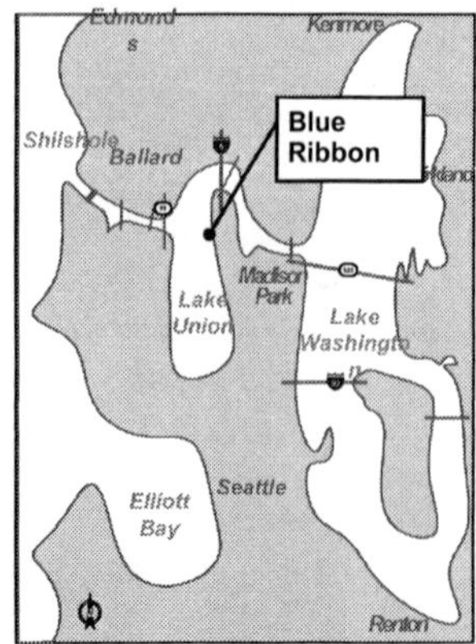

The Blue Ribbon Cooking Culinary Center is conveniently located on the northwest shore of Lake Union and offers beautiful sunset views of the Lake.

The entrance to this secluded hideaway is behind a row of private covered moorage slips. Tie-up space consists of a narrow catwalk along the west side of the building and can accommodate runabouts and small cruisers. Take care walking along the catwalk as it is narrow and is not in the best of repair at this time. Plans include upgrades and repairs to the catwalk in the near future. When arriving by boat, use the entrance to the cooking school on the southwest corner of the building.

BLUE RIBBON GUEST DOCK	
Area	North Lake Union, along the west shore
Address	2501 Fairview Ave E Seattle
Length of Stay	While in Class and Dining
Tie Up Space	Fixed Dock "Cat-Walk" along front (west) side of building
Suitable For	Cruisers, Runabouts
Type	Private
Contact	(206) 328-2442

NORTH LAKE UNION

Blue Ribbon Guest Dock

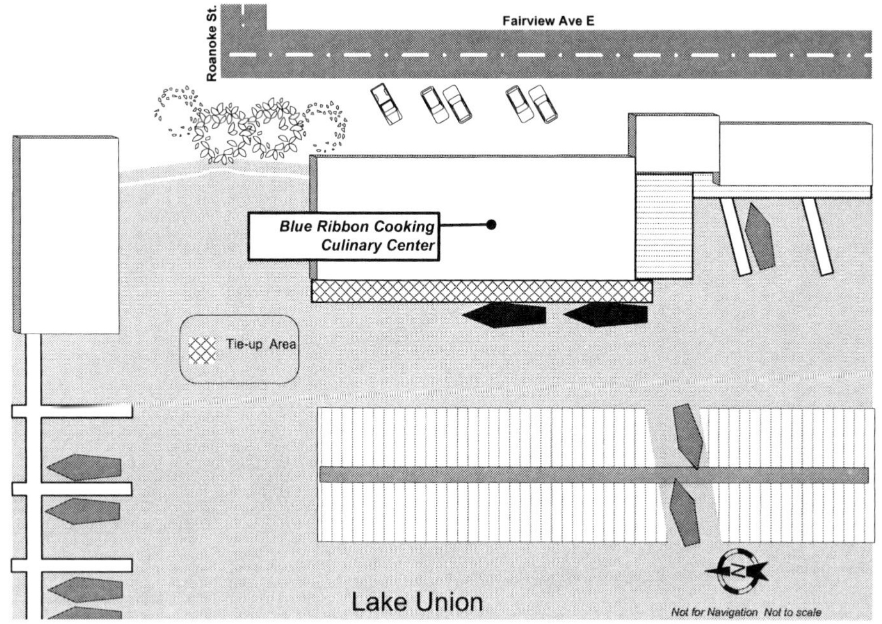

NORTH LAKE UNION

Blue Ribbon Guest Dock

BLUE RIBBON COOKING

Once the site of Café Ambrosia and other restaurants over the years, this venue seems to have found its perfect soul mate, the Blue Ribbon Cooking Culinary Center.

This location offers the boater a truly unique experience. Bring your guests for an evening cooking class and enjoy your dinner creations along with good beers or fine wines. Evening classes are normally three hours long, including the dining experience. Most classes are theme oriented like the Valentine's Menu, Spring Salads Menu, or the Mardi Gras Dinner. There is also a Mother's Day Brunch class and the Perfect Afternoon Tea Class.

Blue Ribbon Cooking is the perfect venue for a corporate or special private event for groups up to 165 people. One instructor is provided for every 10-12 people at various teaching stations on a rotation basis. Don't miss this unique Seattle experience..

Hours	Day Classes: 9am – 4pm Evening Classes: 6:30pm – 10pm
Serving	Brunch, Dinners
Price	$30-$85 per Class
Reservations	Required
Environment	Business Casual
Cuisine	According to Class Schedule
Outdoor Seating	Yes, Deck, Summer Months
Contact Info.	(206) 328-2442 www.BlueRibbonCooking.com
Notables	❑ Classes for Children ❑ Call ahead lunch boxes available to-go

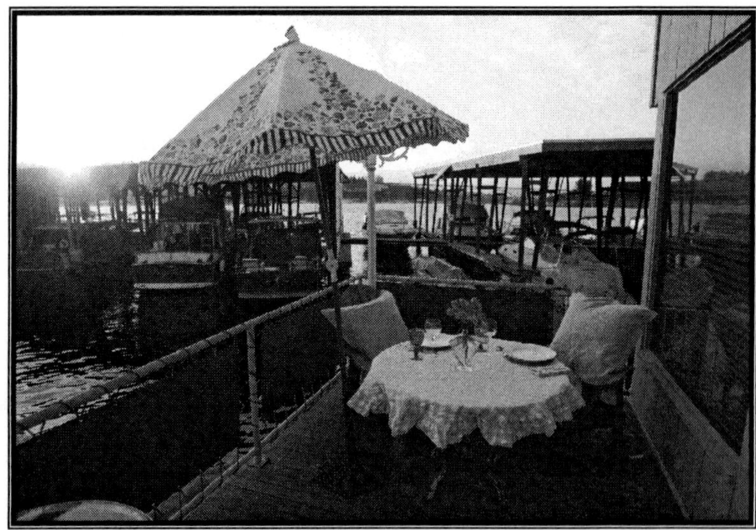

Blue Ribbon Guest Dock

NORTH LAKE UNION
Ivar's Guest Dock

Undoubtedly the Seattle icon of dining by boat, Ivar's Salmon House has been receiving boaters of all kinds for more than 30 years. This restaurant is the lighthouse of destinations for hungry boaters looking for a place to relax indoors or outdoors.

The 60+ feet of floating dock on the west end of the concrete barge will accommodate cruisers, runabouts and paddle craft on both sides. The shore side of the floating dock is a bit too narrow for larger boats and is best suited for runabouts and smaller watercraft.

The concrete barge offers plenty of space to tie-up and there is usually some space available. The 4-5 foot high sides of the barge make this a difficult tie-up space for cruisers or small boats and is best suited for large cruisers and yachts. If the floating dock is full, the barge is always an option but be prepared with extra fenders and a plan to negotiate the concrete sides. Also, your passengers will be grateful if you drop them off on the end of the floating dock before you tie-up to the barge.

This is a popular destination, so on busy weekends and holidays you may need to wait for a space. Rafting is an option here. In consideration of others, use spring lines and tie close to other boats so as to leave space available for other dining boaters.

RESTAURANTS
Ivar's Salmon House
Ivar's Seafood Bar

IVAR'S GUEST DOCK	
Area	North end of Lake Union
Address	401 NE Northlake Way, Seattle
Hours	11am to 10pm
Length of Stay	3 hours
Tie Up Space	60+ feet of floating dock 100+ feet of very high barge
Suitable For	Yachts, Cruisers, Runabouts, Canoes
Type	Private, Ivar's Salmon House
Contact	(206) 632-0767
Fuel	None
Launch	None
Insider Tips	❑ Shore side of float is often overlooked, may have space and is protected from wakes & waves.

NORTH LAKE UNION

Ivar's Guest Dock

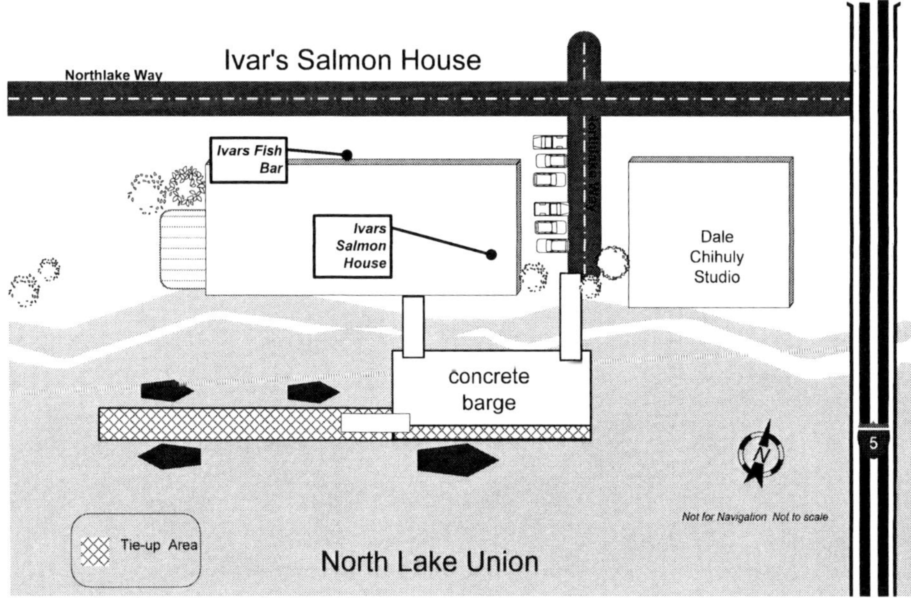

NORTH LAKE UNION

Ivar's Guest Dock

IVAR'S SALMON HOUSE

Ivar's Northwest tradition began in 1938 when Ivar Haglund opened Seattle's first aquarium. He offered his visitors fish'n chips, which began what is now 68 years of Ivar's seafood restaurants. The Ivar's Salmon House has one of the best views on Lake Union looking south towards the Seattle skyline. This is the place to savor Alder smoked Salmon, a northwest tradition not to be missed. Other favorites include Alaskan Halibut, Jumbo Prawn linguini, and the Alaskan True Cod, which is stuffed with Dungeness Crab and Bay Shrimp, baked and topped with mariniere sauce. Ivar's on Lake Union is also a great venue for Sunday Brunch. The restaurant displays native artifacts and beautiful historical photographs of Native Americans. The restaurant building is a replica of a Northwest Indian Longhouse, complete with an Indian-style cooking pit.

Hours	Brunch: 10am - 2pm Sundays Lunch: 11am - 4pm Mon-Sat Dinner: 4pm - 9pm Mon-Thur 4pm - 10pm Fri-Sat 3:30pm - 9pm Sundays Lounge: 11am – 11pm Mon-Sat 10am – 11pm Sundays
Serving	Brunch, Lunch, Dinner
Price	$20 Brunch $8-$16 Lunch $12-$28 Dinner
Reservations	Recommended
Cuisine	Seafood, Chicken, Prime Rib
Outdoor Seating	Yes
Contact Info.	(206) 632-0767 www.ivars.net
Notables	❑ Established by historic Seattle figure, Ivar Hagland ❑ Complimentary snacks 2pm-3:30pm in the lounge on Sun ❑ Lavish Sunday Brunch.

NORTH LAKE UNION
Ivar's Guest Dock

IVAR'S SEAFOOD BAR

To find the seafood bar, walk from the barge over the little bridge past the main restaurant and out to the street, turn left and you will find the bar on the street-side of the building. Serving Ivar's famous clam chowder, fish'n chips, alder-smoked salmon, and other delicious food for casual dining, makes this take-out bar a favorite among locals as well as tourists. The procedure for ordering at the window is to holler out your fish or chicken order, don't worry about the drinks, you take care of that when you pay. If you are unsure of the procedure, ask a local; they are more than happy to help. Year-round indoor seating is available next to the take-out bar or you can dine at tables on the floating barge and enjoy the great view of Seattle.

Hours	Lunch/Dinner 11am - 10pm Mon-Thurs 11am - 11pm Fri-Sat
Serving	Lunch, Dinner
Price	$5-$10
Reservations	No
Cuisine	Seafood and Chicken take out
Outdoor Seating	Yes, (indoor year-round seating is also available)
Contact Info.	(206) 632-0767 www.ivarsrestaurants.com
Notables	❑ Indian Style Smoked Salmon is available as take out

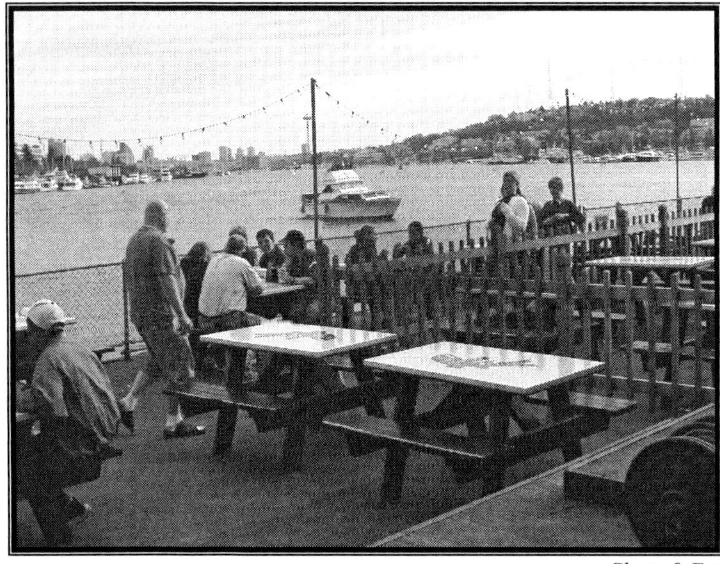

NORTH LAKE UNION

Terry Pettus Park

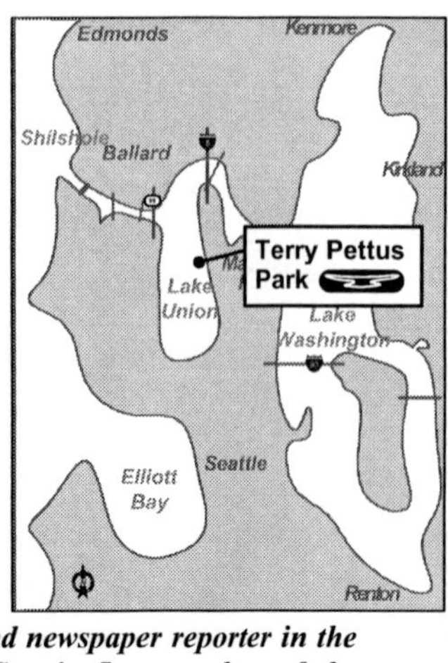

This street end park, suitable for small runabouts and canoes, is almost hidden among the houseboats on Lake Union and is one of those landings that will set you apart from other boating diners. Boaters may tie-up at the dock for 2 hours and have a choice of three restaurants within a short walk of the park.

Look for the NOAA ships on the east central area of Lake Union. You will see several large pilings perpendicular to the shore. Follow the channel between the houseboats and the pilings eastward to the Terry Pettus dock.

This street-end park was named in honor of Terry Pettus, who lived from 1904 to 1984 and was an active political leader and newspaper reporter in the Seattle area. He became Washington State's first member of the American Newspaper Guild and he was a key organizer of the Seattle chapter. In his latter years, Terry and his wife Berta lived in a houseboat on Lake Union and Terry Pettus helped form the Lake Union Houseboat Owners Association, now called the "Floating Homes Association." He was also instrumental in helping clean up Lake Union. At that time, houseboats had no sewer lines and the City of Seattle had 13 sewer outflows directly into Lake Union. The Terry Pettus Park reflects the namesake's desire to help create a sharing society.

When approaching the float, please respect the quiet privacy of the adjacent houseboats.

RESTAURANTS
Azteca
Serafina
Siam Thai Cuisine

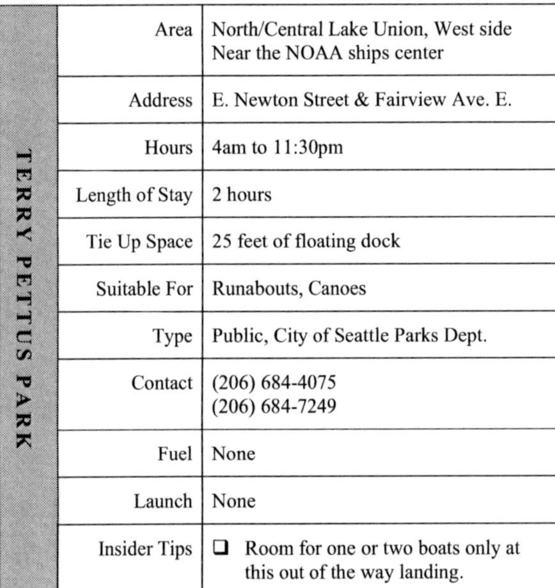

TERRY PETTUS PARK	
Area	North/Central Lake Union, West side Near the NOAA ships center
Address	E. Newton Street & Fairview Ave. E.
Hours	4am to 11:30pm
Length of Stay	2 hours
Tie Up Space	25 feet of floating dock
Suitable For	Runabouts, Canoes
Type	Public, City of Seattle Parks Dept.
Contact	(206) 684-4075 (206) 684-7249
Fuel	None
Launch	None
Insider Tips	❑ Room for one or two boats only at this out of the way landing.

NORTH LAKE UNION
Terry Pettus Park

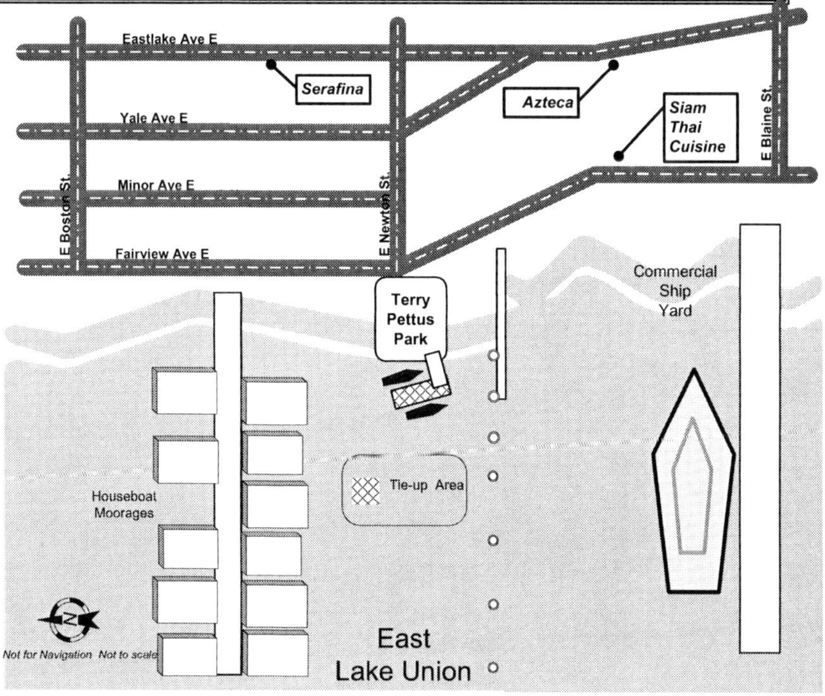

Eastlake Ave E
Serafina
Azteca
Siam Thai Cuisine
Yale Ave E
E Blaine St.
Minor Ave E
E Boston St.
E Newton St.
Fairview Ave E
Commercial Ship Yard
Terry Pettus Park
Tie-up Area
Houseboat Moorages
Not for Navigation Not to scale
East Lake Union

NORTH LAKE UNION
Terry Pettus Park

AZTECA MEXICAN

The Azteca is about three blocks from the Terry Pettus Park Dock. From the park walk east on E. Newton Street and turn right on Yale Place. Follow Yale Place to the restaurant at 1823 Eastlake Ave. East. Azteca restaurants are a family owned business and serve traditional Mexican recipes like Tacos, Enchiladas, Tostadas, and Spanish omelettes. Chef specials include Arroz con Pollo, which is chicken prepared with mushrooms, onions, peppers, and cheese with their special sauce and garnished with avocado and tomato. The Camarones Mexicanos is prepared in the same manner, replacing the chicken with shrimp. During the hot summer months, you can enjoy the tree-shaded outdoor deck while sipping a Margarita and other refreshing beverages.

Hours	Lunch: 11am - 3pm Mon-Fri Dinner: 3pm - 10pm Sun-Thur 3pm - 11pm Fri-Sat
Serving	Lunch, Dinner
Price	$7-$10 Lunch $8-$14 Dinner
Reservations	Recommended
Environment	Casual
Cuisine	Chicken, Seafood, Beef, Enchiladas, Tostadas, Tacos, Burritos
Outdoor Seating	Yes, Deck, Summer Months
Contact Info.	(206) 324-4941 www.aztecamex.com

SERAFINA RESTAURANT

The Serafina Restaurant is about three blocks from the Terry Pettus Park Dock. From the park, walk east on E. Newton Street until you reach Eastlake Ave. E. and turn left to the restaurant at 2043 Eastlake Ave. E. Serafina's charming romantic ambiance makes this restaurant a perfect place to bring a date. Jazz groups and Latin ensembles entertain patrons on Fridays, Saturdays, and Sundays and the first Wednesday of each month. Serafina serves country Italian fare and has a fresh supply of herbs and edible flowers in the nearby Kitchen Garden. Try the house-made misto di salsiccia, a generous plate of sausages over creamy grilled polenta or the Melanzane alla Serafina, their signature dish of thinly sliced eggplant rolled with ricotta cheese, fresh basil, and parmesan baked in a tomato sauce served over cappellini.

Hours	Lunch: 11:30am - 2:30pm Mon-Fri Dinner:: 5:30pm - 10pm Sun-Thur 5:30pm - 11pm Fri-Sat
Serving	Lunch, Dinner
Price	$8-$13 Lunch $9-$24 Dinner
Reservations	Recommended
Environment	Business Casual / Dressy
Cuisine	Veal, Rabbit, Pastas, Vegetables
Outdoor Seating	Yes, Patio, Summer Months
Contact Info.	(206) 323-0807 www.serafinaseattle.com
Notables	❑ On-line Reservations ❑ Serafina Merchandise

SIAM THAI CUISINE

The Siam Thai is about two blocks from the Terry Pettus Park Dock. Turn right from the head of the park and walk south-east on Fairview Ave. E. The restaurant is on the left-hand side at 1880 Fairview Ave. East. Siam has long been known as one of the best Thai cuisine restaurants in Seattle. The authentic Thai dishes come with friendly service and generous portions. Favorite entrees include garlic prawns, pad Thai, and Siam special orange beef. Siam Thai has two other locations in Seattle on Broadway and Queen Anne Hill. The Lake Union location has created a rustic venue with its train boxcar sides used as outdoor paneling.

Hours	Lunch: 11:30am - 3pm Mon-Fri Dinner: 3pm - 10pm Mon-Thur 3pm - 11pm Fri & Sat 5pm – 10pm Sundays
Serving	Lunch, Dinner
Price	$7-$9 Lunch $8-$14 Dinner
Reservations	Recommended
Environment	Casual
Cuisine	Seafood, Chicken, Beef, Noodles, Vegetables
Outdoor Seating	Yes, Small Deck, Summers
Contact Info.	(206) 323-8101 siamlakeunion.citysearch.com

South Lake Union

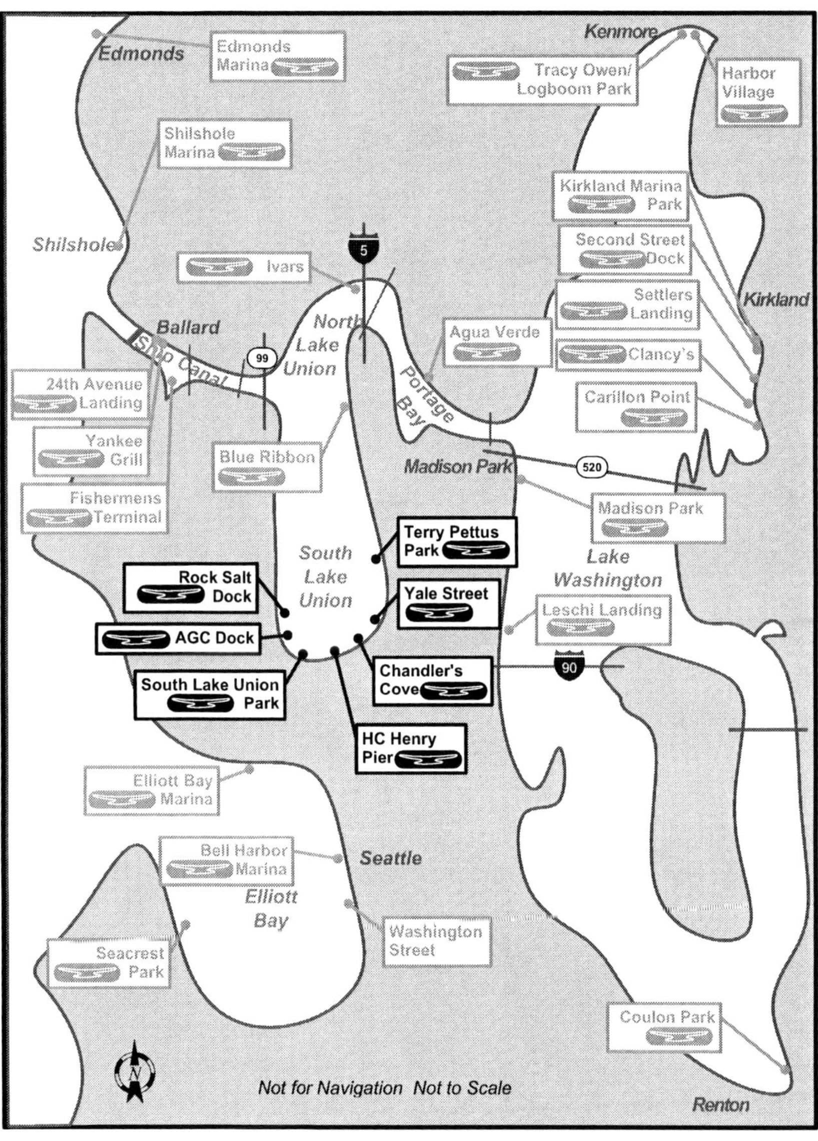
Edmonds
Edmonds Marina
Kenmore
Tracy Owen/ Logboom Park
Harbor Village
Shilshole Marina
Kirkland Marina Park
Shilshole
Second Street Dock
Ivars
5
Settlers Landing
Kirkland
North Lake Union
Agua Verde
Ballard
Ship Canal
99
Clancy's
24th Avenue Landing
Portage Bay
Carillon Point
Yankee Grill
Blue Ribbon
Madison Park
520
Fishermens Terminal
Madison Park
Terry Pettus Park
South Lake Union
Lake Washington
Rock Salt Dock
Yale Street
Leschi Landing
AGC Dock
Chandler's Cove
90
South Lake Union Park
HC Henry Pier
Elliott Bay Marina
Bell Harbor Marina
Seattle
Elliott Bay
Seacrest Park
Washington Street
Coulon Park
Not for Navigation Not to Scale
Renton

SOUTH LAKE UNION
AGC Building Guest Dock

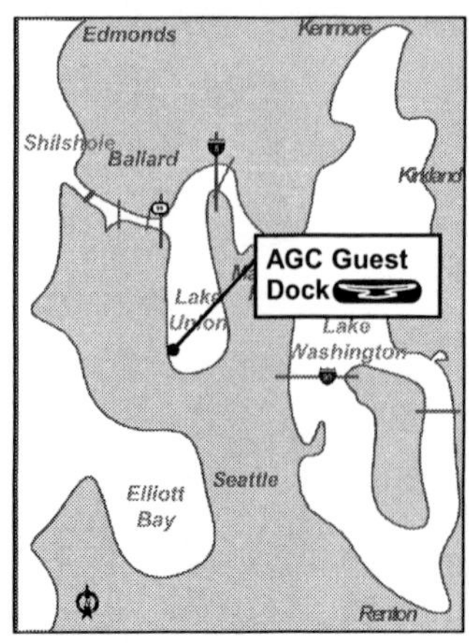

The AGC Building is one of the tallest buildings on the south end of Lake Union, and its unmistakable "AGC" in big gold letters on each side, make it an excellent landmark. The building offers tie-up space for guests at McCormick & Schmick's Harborside Restaurant and Starbucks Coffee.

RESTAURANTS
McCormick & Schmick's Harborside
Starbucks Coffee

The tie-up area, located on the south side of the building, offers up to 85' of space and is well protected from wind and waves. The restaurant and coffee shop is only a few steps from the tie-up area.

AGC GUEST DOCK	
Area	Southwest shore of Lake Union
Address	1200 Westlake Ave North, Seattle
Length of Stay	No Overnight Stays
Tie Up Space	85 feet of medium high dock
Suitable For	Cruisers, Runabouts
Type	Private, AGC Building
Insider Tips	❑ Tie-up area is "First-come First Serve" and no-reserving – no exceptions

SOUTH LAKE UNION

AGC Building Guest Dock

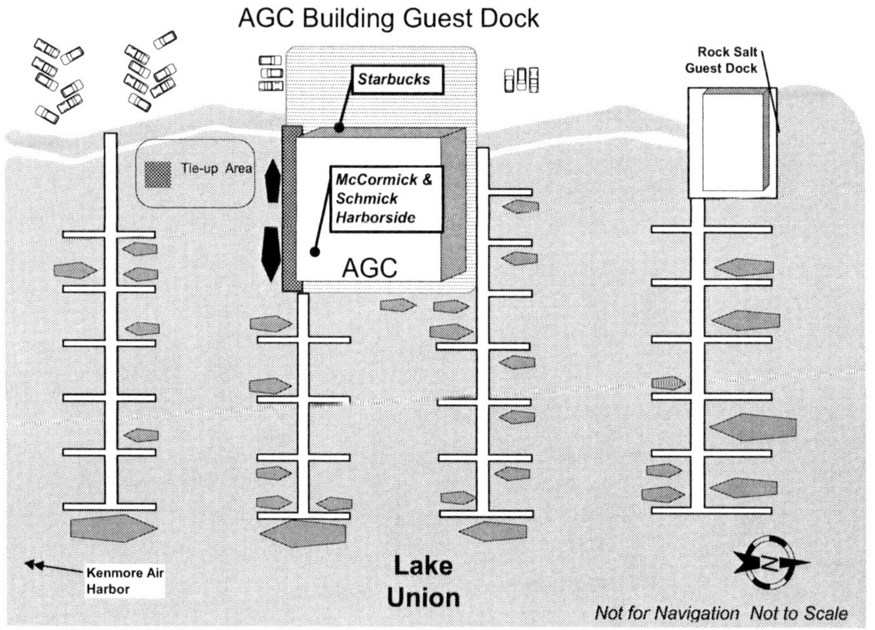

SOUTH LAKE UNION
AGC Building Guest Dock

MCCORMICK & SCHMICK'S HARBORSIDE

McCormick & Schmick's restaurants are well known on the West Coast and maintain a high standard. This nice restaurant with its warm woods and high ceilings offers a wide selection of fresh fish, including Oregon Petrale Sole, Trout, Salmon, Alaskan Halibut, and Hawaiian Albacore. Entrée choices also include steaks, chicken, and Game Hen. Specialties include the Thresher Shark blackened with rum butter sauce and tropical fruit salsa. The Columbia River Sturgeon seared and served over Granny Smith Apples with sweet potatoes and bacon is another favorite. McCormick & Schmick's Harborside has one of the best views of Lake Union and the Seattle cityscape from its outside deck and upper level restaurant and deck. The two lively bars, one located upstairs and the other downstairs, offer high quality liquors and wines. A large selection of beers and other beverages are also available.

Hours	Lunch: 11:30am - 3:30pm Mon-Fri Sat & Sun 11:30am – 3:30pm May through August Dinner:: 4pm - 10pm Sun-Thur 4pm - 11pm Fri & Sat
Serving	Lunch, Dinner
Price	$7-$14 Lunch $7-$24 Dinner
Reservations	Recommended
Environment	Business Casual / Dressy
Cuisine	Seafood, Chicken, Pasta, Salads
Outdoor Seating	Yes, Deck(s), Summer Months
Contact Info.	(206) 270-9052 www.mccormickandschmicks.com
Notables	❑ Two Bars ❑ Brunch Items on Menu ❑ Banquet Services ❑ Catering

SOUTH LAKE UNION
AGC Building Guest Dock

STARBUCKS COFFEE

This Starbucks location is worth a special note regarding the great views of Lake Union and the City skyline from both inside the shop and from the summer patio. This location also stays open later than some of the other Starbucks locations. Starbucks continues to expand with new shops and this site is one of the newest in the Seattle area. The very first Starbucks opened in 1971 at Seattle's Pike Place Market, which has become a must see among Starbucks fans. The AGC location is a quick easy stop for the boater in need of a hot cup of coffee.

Hours	5am – 10pm Mon-Fri 6am – 8pm Sat & Sun
Serving	Coffee, Cookies, Pastries
Price	$3 - $7
Reservations	No
Outdoor Seating	Yes, Patio, Summer Months
Contact Info.	(206) 216-0306
Notables	❑ Nice View

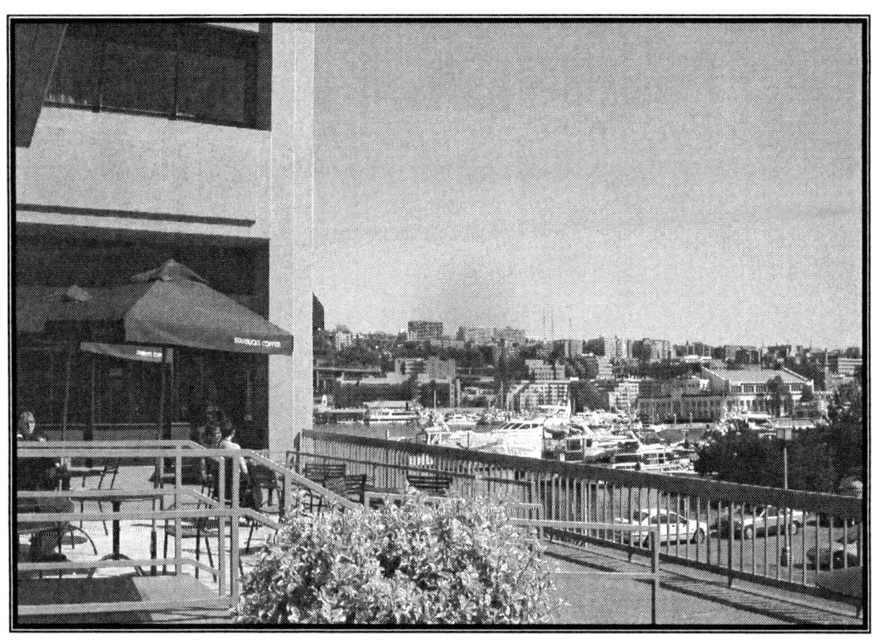

SOUTH LAKE UNION

Chandler's Cove Guest Dock

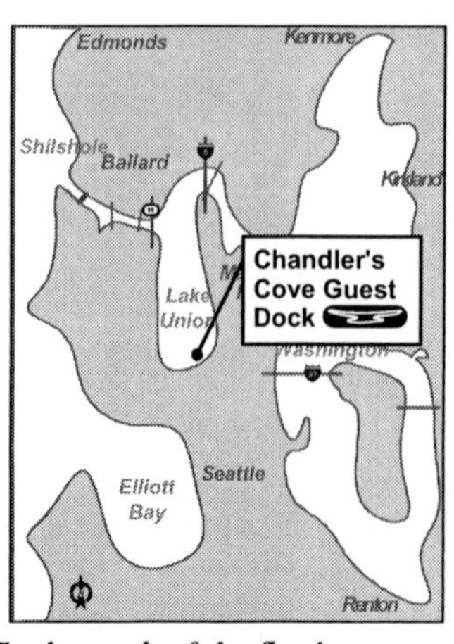

Chandler's Cove has a large wharf on the south end of Lake Union, which serves five restaurants. Tie-up space is available for customers visiting Chandler's Cove restaurants and merchants.

Chandler's Cove wharf has two tie-up areas. The 40'x20' float at the North (deep water) end of the wharf is a good spot for day-cruisers and smaller craft. There is limited space on this float with room for only 3 or so boats. If the 40' face of the float is full, smaller runabouts with skilled skippers can tie-up on the ends of this float. To the south of the floating dock extending to the shoreline, the west side of the wharf offers 150 feet of high tie-up area. Excursion ships and a variety of other large vessels normally use this area. If you have a smaller boat, you can often slip into a space between the big-boys in this area.

The attractive plaza, shops, and restaurants at Chandler's Cove are a popular draw for boaters. It is best to arrive early on Friday or Saturday evenings during prime boating season.

RESTAURANTS
Chandler's Crabhouse
Daniels Broiler (See H.C. Henry Pier)
Duke's Chowder House
Hooters
Joeys

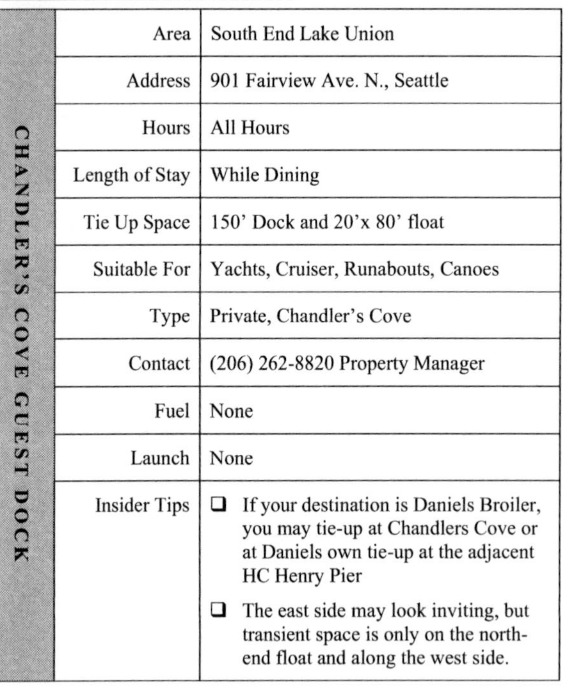

CHANDLER'S COVE GUEST DOCK	
Area	South End Lake Union
Address	901 Fairview Ave. N., Seattle
Hours	All Hours
Length of Stay	While Dining
Tie Up Space	150' Dock and 20'x 80' float
Suitable For	Yachts, Cruiser, Runabouts, Canoes
Type	Private, Chandler's Cove
Contact	(206) 262-8820 Property Manager
Fuel	None
Launch	None
Insider Tips	❑ If your destination is Daniels Broiler, you may tie-up at Chandlers Cove or at Daniels own tie-up at the adjacent HC Henry Pier ❑ The east side may look inviting, but transient space is only on the north-end float and along the west side.

SOUTH LAKE UNION
Chandler's Cove Guest Dock

HC Henry Pier
Chandler's Cove Guest Dock
Joeys
Hooters
Dukes
Chandler's
Yale Street Landing
Tie-up Area
Lake Union
Not for Navigation Not to scale

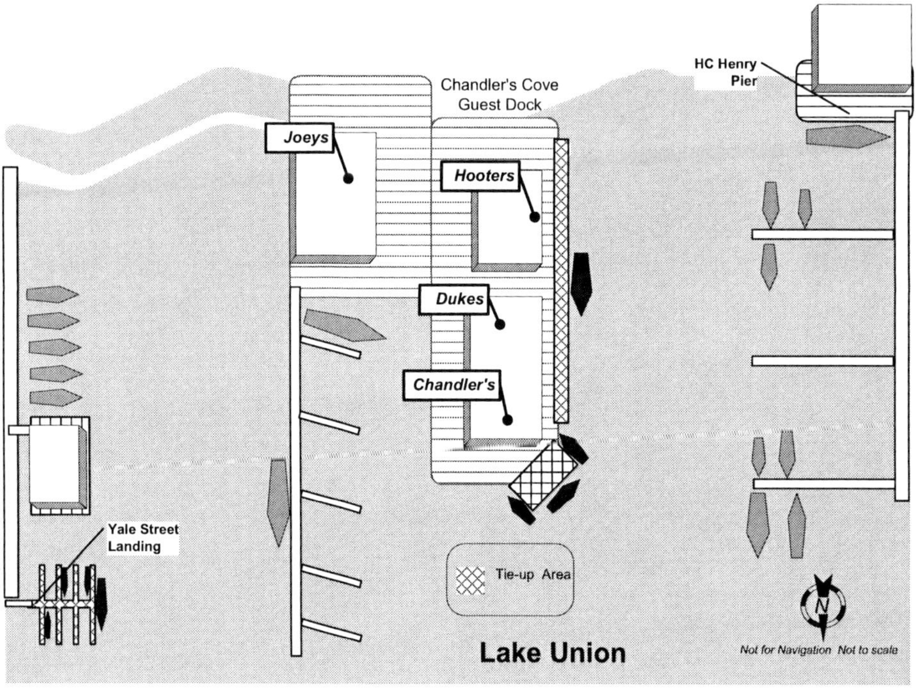

SOUTH LAKE UNION
Chandler's Cove Guest Dock

CHANDLER'S CRABHOUSE

Chandler's Crabhouse offers a wide variety of fresh crab and other seafood dishes year-round. For dinner try the Australian Rock Lobster Tail with saffron risotto, grilled asparagus, and lemon butter sauce or try the Ginger Smoked Sturgeon cedar planked with roasted root vegetables, braised greens, and roasted pepper coulis. Salads, soups, and seafood entrees are offered at lunch. Chandler's new lounge has been redesigned to take advantage of the great views and seating is available during the summers on the large deck with umbrella cover to enjoy the seaplanes, boats, and Lake Union views. Box lunches and platters are available through Gretchen's Shoebox Express by calling (206) 623-8194.

Hours	Brunch: 10am - 3pm Sat & Sun Lunch: 11am - 3pm Mon-Fri Dinner: 5pm – 10pm Sun-Thur 5pm – 11pm Fri & Sat Lounge: Closes Midnight Sun-Wed Closes 1:30am Fri & Sat
Serving	Brunch, Lunch, Dinner
Price	$13-$22 Brunch / Lunch $16-$37 Dinner
Reservations	Recommended
Environment	Business Casual / Dressy
Cuisine	Seafood
Outdoor Seating	Yes, Bar Deck on the east side Dinner Deck on north side
Contact Info.	(206) 223-2722 schwartzbrothersrestaurants.com
Notables	❑ On-line Reservations ❑ "Crabby Hour" Specials

JOEYS

Cucina Cucina restaurants have started a new concept dining experience called Joeys now housed in the former Cucina restaurant. This sheik night-life restaurant sports the latest color scheme of brown and black tones on the tables, walls, leather chairs, and tile floors. Porthole style lighting in the foyer and ship helm style windows in the bar area create soft background lighting. Cozy corner window areas take advantage of the Lake Union views. The summer deck has comfortable high-back patio chairs and attractive stone-topped tables. Joeys serves a wide variety of dishes, including beef, chicken, pork, seafood, sandwiches, and burgers. The full menu is available until 1:30 a.m. daily.

Hours	Dinner: 11am – 2am Daily Full menu until 1:30am
Serving	Dinner
Price	$10 - $30
Reservations	No (Can call ahead for status)
Environment	Hip Casual
Cuisine	Beef, Chicken, Pork, Seafood
Outdoor Seating	Yes, Deck, Summer Months
Contact Info.	(206) 749-5639 www.joeysrestaurants.com
Notables	❑ To-Go Orders at Dock Side

SOUTH LAKE UNION
Chandler's Cove Guest Dock

DUKE'S CHOWDER HOUSE

Duke's, a Seattle icon for more than 25 years, is a great place to be, to enjoy a hot bowl of chowder on a cold, rainy Seattle day. Complete with a fireplace and picnic-style tables covered with blue and white tablecloths, you can choose from a wide selection of chowders, including clam, crayfish, crab & Bourbon, Salmon, shrimp, Cajun Chicken, Lobster, and Duke's Northwest Seafood Chowder. If you find it difficult to choose just one, try the Chowder Sampler. No, not everyday in Seattle is a cold day, so Duke's offers a nice selection of pastas, seafood, burgers, steaks, and salads. Duke's also has a full service bar with a good selection of beer, wine, and featured "Duketails" – cocktails. Enjoy the open deck during the warm summer months with nice views of Lake Union along with your favorite beverage.

Hours	Lunch/Dinner: 11:30am - Midnight Daily Dinner menu begins at 3pm Bar stays open till 2am
Serving	Lunch, Dinner
Price	$7-$15 Lunch $10-$20 Dinner
Reservations	Recommended
Environment	Casual
Cuisine	Chowders, Seafood, Pasta, Burgers, Salads
Outdoor Seating	Yes, Deck, Summer Months
Contact Info.	(206) 382-9963 www.dukeschowderhouse.com

HOOTERS

In 1983, six fun loving businessmen, with no previous restaurant experience, opened a Clearwater, Florida joint with girls in orange shorts serving chicken wings. Now a corporation, Hooters of America is an Atlanta-based franchiser. The casual beach-theme features '50s and '60s jukebox music and televisions for viewing sporting events. The element of female sex appeal is prevalent and a large percentage of the patrons are males. Hooters offers a nice selection of appetizers, sandwiches, salads, and their signature chicken wings.

Hours	11am - 12pm Mon-Thurs 11am - 1pm Fri-Sat 11am - 11pm Sundays
Serving	Lunch, Dinner
Price	$7-$20
Reservations	No (Yes, parties of 15 or more)
Environment	Casual
Cuisine	Chicken, Sandwiches, Salads
Outdoor Seating	No
Contact Info.	(206) 625-0555 www.hooters.com
Notables	❑ Hooters Logo Merchandise

SOUTH LAKE UNION
H.C. Henry Pier

Guests of Daniels Broiler restaurant may tie-up at the H.C. Henry Pier. H.C. Henry Pier is the complex housing Daniels Broiler on Lake Union. Guest Moorage is located on the south side of the southern most (nearest shore) finger pier to the West of the main pier.

RESTAURANT	
	Daniels Broiler

To find the guest moorage, locate the Wooden Boat Center on the south end of Lake Union and navigate the channel immediately to the east of the Wooden Boat Center to the shoreline and then turn east. The tie-up area is only on the south (shore) side of the last finger pier. Look for a small "Guest Moorage" sign on the end of the pier and large "H.C. Henry" sign at the head of the pier. If space here is not available, you may also use the Chandler's Cove Dock while dining at Daniel's.

H.C. HENRY PIER		
	Area	South Lake Union, east of Wooden Boat Center
	Address	809 Fairview Place North
	Length of Stay	Maximum 3 hours
	Tie Up Space	75 feet of floating dock Guest area on south side only
	Suitable For	Yachts, Cruisers, Runabouts
	Type	Private, H.C. Henry Pier
	Contact	(206) 262-8820
	Insider Tips	❑ Guest Moorage on south side of finger pier

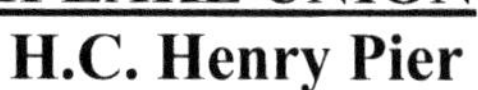

SOUTH LAKE UNION
H.C. Henry Pier

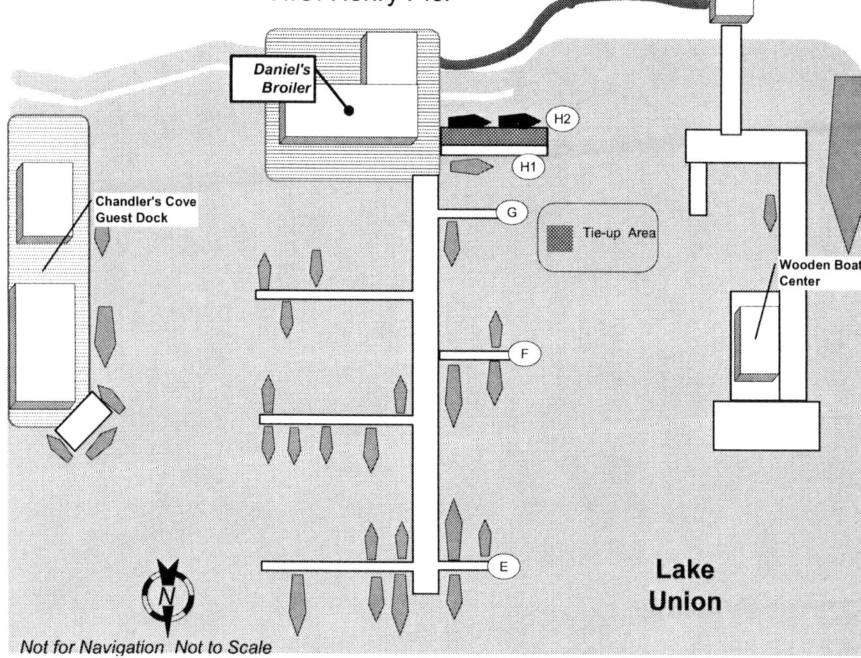

SOUTH LAKE UNION
H.C. Henry Pier

DANIELS BROILER

For the steak lover, Daniels prepares the perfect steak using only the top two percent prime cuts. Your steak is carefully trimmed and placed under a special broiler to lock in the flavor and juices. Quality steaks include the Filet Mignon, Rib-Eye, Porterhouse, Top Sirloin, and the New York, which are served with your choice of mashed garlic potatoes, baked potato, or rice and fresh broccoli. Other delicious choices at Daniel's include fresh seafood, chicken, and veal. Dining on the deck is available during the summer months overlooking the marinas and Chandler's Cove. Enjoy live entertainment in the piano bar, which is open daily during evening hours. This classy and beautifully appointed restaurant is every steak lover's favorite. Daniels is now open for lunch Monday through Friday.

Hours	Lunch: 11:30am – 2:30pm Mon-Fri Dinner: 5pm - 10pm Sun-Thur 5pm - 11pm Fri & Sat Happy Hour: 4pm - 6:30pm Daily
Serving	Lunch, Dinner
Price	$26-$36
Reservations	Recommended
Environment	Business Casual
Cuisine	Steaks, Seafood, Chicken, Veal
Outdoor Seating	Yes, Deck, Summer Months
Contact Info.	(206) 621-8262 www.swartzbrothersrestaurants.com
Notables	❑ Live Entertainment

Enjoy the trip even
when plans change.

SOUTH LAKE UNION
H.C. Henry Pier

SOUTH LAKE UNION
Rock Salt Guest Dock

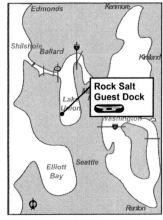

The Rock Salt Steak House is an excellent option for dining at the south end of Lake Union and offers moorage for boating diners on two docks located along the east and north sides of the building. The restaurant is easy to find and boating access to the moorage area is open.

RESTAURANT	
	Rock Salt Steak House

Rock Salt is located a few hundred feet north of the AGC building. Look for the wide channel that lines up with the big red brick "Casey Family Building" on Queen Anne Hill. At the end of the channel is the Rock Salt Steak House.

The entrance to the restaurant is on the shore side of the building. There's nothing complicated about this landing, making it an easy dining destination for boaters.

ROCK SALT GUEST DOCK		
	Area	Southwest End of Lake Union
	Address	1232 Westlake Ave N., Seattle
	Hours	Restaurant Hours
	Length of Stay	While Dining
	Tie Up Space	90 feet of fixed dock on north 75 feet of floating dock on west
	Suitable For	Yachts, Cruisers, Runabouts
	Type	Private, Rock Salt Restaurant
	Insider Tips	❑ Line up with the brick "Casey Family Building"

SOUTH LAKE UNION
Rock Salt Guest Dock

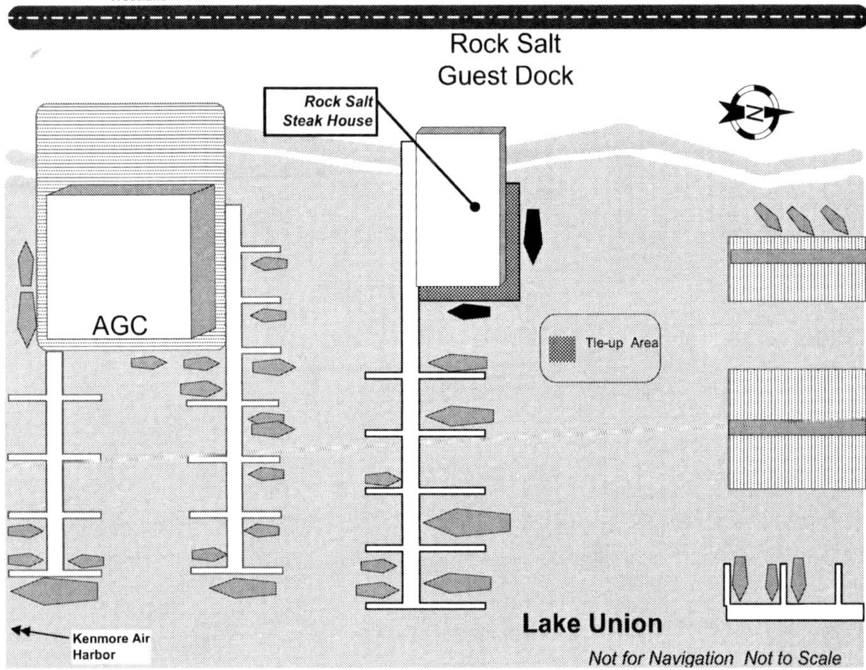

SOUTH LAKE UNION
Rock Salt Guest Dock

ROCK SALT STEAK HOUSE

This quiet, relaxing restaurant is located at the end of a short channel and has a pleasant view of Lake Union with private marinas in the foreground. Recent updates to the restaurant include a new outdoor deck for summer dining and a new large bar area. The Rock Salt restaurant is known for its prime rib, which is roasted very slowly covered in a blanket of coarse rock salt. Delicious char grilled steaks are also served, including the Chicago Rib Eye, New York, and the Top Sirloin. The Rock Salt goes beyond steaks and offers a nice selection of fresh seafood dishes and creative salads. Dinner entrees are served with fresh lemon spinach and garlic mashed potatoes. Lunch items include sandwiches, burgers, and pasta along with steak and seafood dishes. The Rock Salt Steak House is a nice choice for brunch. Egg dishes and omelets are served with hash-browns and toast. Pancakes and waffles are also offered.

Hours	Brunch: 11am – 3pm Sundays Lunch: 11am - 3pm Daily Dinner: 3pm – 10pm Sun-Thur 3pm – 11pm Fri & Sat
Serving	Brunch, Lunch, Dinner
Price	$8-$15 Breakfast and Lunch $16-$25 Dinner
Reservations	Recommended
Environment	Casual / Business Casual
Cuisine	Seafood, Pasta, Steak, Salads
Outdoor Seating	No (Yes, banquet facilities)
Contact Info.	(206) 284-1047 www.rocksaltonlatitude47.com

Make reservations
whenever you can.

SOUTH LAKE UNION

Rock Salt Guest Dock

SOUTH LAKE UNION
South Lake Union Park

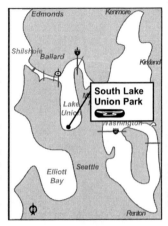

With the addition of the Naval Reserve building and surrounding land to this City of Seattle park, the South Lake Union Park consists of 16 acres of land. Evolution and enhancement to this location continues to benefit the public.

The small float/dock along the west shore just south of the Kenmore Air dock is available for day use without charge for a maximum stay of 4 hours. Although a posted sign upland in the Park states that the float is for non-motorized boats and must not be left unattended, small powerboats (runabouts and dingys) may dock at the float for short stays per the Seattle Parks Department. Several good restaurants are within easy walking distance of the float/dock.

RESTAURANTS
Bonefish Grill
Buca Di Bepo
Jillian's Billiard Club
Outback Steakhouse

The Naval Reserve building is currently under the management of the Maritime Heritage Foundation and uses the old naval base docks for historic ships and educational purposes. Future plans include tie-up space for the public, possibly by 2007. The Naval Reserve dock will be an ideal landing for the restaurants nearby. The Center for Wooden Boats is also considering providing guest space for canoes and kayaks sometime in the near future.

SOUTH LAKE UNION PARK	
Area	South Lake Union
Address	860 Terry Ave. N.
Hours	Daylight Hours
Length of Stay	4 hours
Tie Up Space	10x20 foot floating dock 200+ feet of high fixed bulkhead (Naval)
Suitable For	Canoes, Runabouts
Type	Public, City of Seattle Parks Dept.
Contact	(206) 684-7031 Victoria (206) 684-4075 (206) 684-7249

For the current status regarding the development of the park and related docks, call Victoria, Project Manager, at 206-684-7031 at the City of Seattle. Boaters are encouraged to call the City to promote further development of the park to include additional public boat access.

SOUTH LAKE UNION

South Lake Union Park

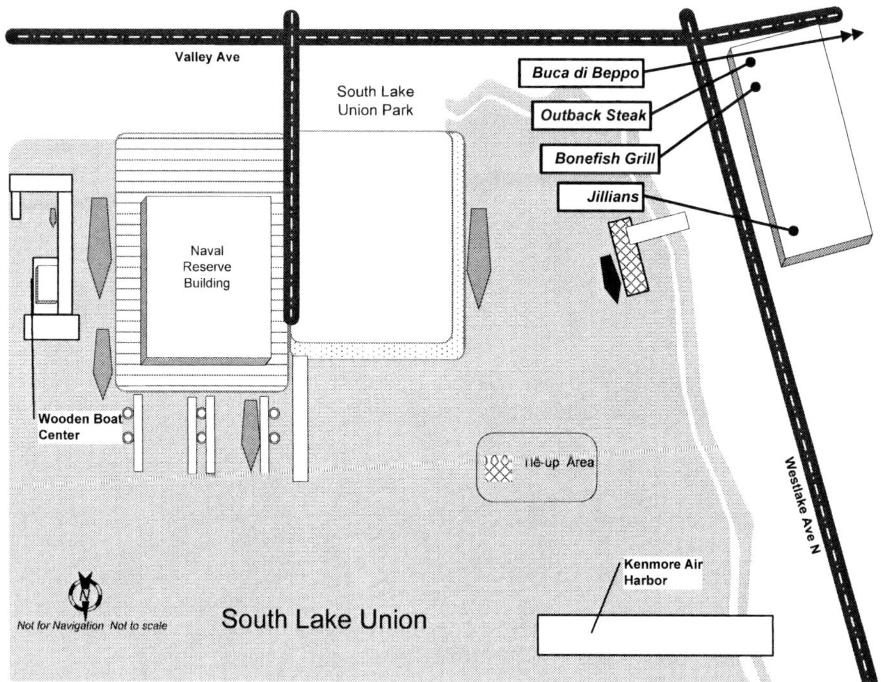

SOUTH LAKE UNION
South Lake Union Park

BONEFISH GRILL

The Bonefish is located at 711 Westlake Ave. N. across the street from the South Lake Union Park and guest dock. The Bonefish Grill specializes in fresh seafood with servers who have the expertise to help you choose the type of fish, preparation, flavors, and sauces to match your taste preference. The Hawaiian Ahi Tuna, Idaho Rainbow Trout, Chilean Sea Bass and other fish choices are cooked over a wood burning grill which fills the restaurant with its delicious aroma. Additional menu items include steak, chicken, and pasta dishes. The Bonefish is visually attractive, as well, with yellow stucco walls displaying beautiful metal sculptures with soft back lighting and linen set tables. The separate bar room is an extension of the restaurant with candle-lit tall bar style tables.

Hours	Lunch: 11:30am – 3pm Mon-Fri Dinner: 4pm – 10:30pm Mon-Thur 4pm – 11:30pm Fri & Sat 4pm – 10pm Sundays
Serving	Lunch, Dinner
Price	$15 - $20
Reservations	Recommended
Environment	Business Casual / Dressy
Cuisine	Seafood, Steak, Chicken
Outdoor Seating	No
Contact Info.	(206) 405-2663

BUCA DI BEPPO

Buca di Beppo serves southern Italian fare on large family platters meant to be shared. Exuberant portions of chicken cacciatore, veal parmigiana, garlic mashed potatoes, pasta dishes, and salads spill over the serving trays. The wood fired thin crust Neapolitan pizzas are especially good. For the lighter appetite, ask for the Buca per Due (for two), which is perfect for smaller parties. All of the wines at Beppo's are Italian and most are special ordered. The décor is as vibrant as the food with a fun whimsical combination of Rococo, Italian, Greek, and American icons. You and your party will definitely have fun at Buca di Beppo ("Joe's basement") with its adventure-some series of dinning rooms and its Italian community atmosphere. Buca di Beppo is located behind the Bonefish Grill on the corner of 9th N. and Roy.

Hours	Dinner: 5pm – 10pm Mon-Thur 5pm – 11pm Fridays Noon – 11pm Saturdays Noon – 10pm Sundays
Serving	Dinner
Price	$12 - $24
Reservations	Recommended / Special Rooms
Environment	Casual
Cuisine	Pastas, Pizzas, Chicken, Veal
Outdoor Seating	No
Contact Info.	(206) 244-2288 www.bucadibeppo.com
Notables	❑ Lunch Sat & Sun Only

SOUTH LAKE UNION
South Lake Union Park

JILLIAN'S BILLIARD CLUB

Juillian's, located just across the street from the South Lake Union Park and guest dock at 731 Westlake Ave. N., combines entertainment with American food favorites. The two-story building has high ceilings with drop lighting and large windows overlooking Lake Union. Both levels house numerous pool tables and TV monitors. The downstairs electronic game room is another popular entertainment spot for groups and individuals alike. The Lake view dining room, located next to the beverage bar, is transformed into a dance floor during the evening hours. You will like the variety of food offered on the menu as well, including soups, salads, burgers, ribs, pizza, chicken, and fish. Jillian's is a fun dining venue any time of day.

Hours	LunchDinner: 11am – 2am Mon-Fri 12pm – 2am Sat & Sun
Serving	Lunch, Dinner
Price	$8 - $13
Reservations	Yes, parties of 8 or more
Environment	Casual
Cuisine	Burgers, Chicken, Fish, Pizza
Outdoor Seating	No
Contact Info.	(206) 223-0300 www.jillians.com
Notables	❑ 32 Billiard Tables

OUTBACK STEAKHOUSE

The Outback Steak House, located at 701 Westlake Ave. N., has a rustic outback appeal with an Aussie theme décor of boomerangs, kangaroos, and the like. Wood-plank, half-height walls define the dining spaces downstairs. The upstairs consists of several dining areas, a separate bar, and a patio area with great views of Lake Union. The Outback offers a wide variety of dishes from lamb, beef, and pork to chicken, fish, and pasta. Try the Outback Rack, a 14 oz. rack of New Zealand lamb served with Cabernet sauce and choice of salad or try the Jackeroo Chops, two 8 oz. center cut port chops served with cinnamon apples and roasted garlic mashed potatoes. Don't miss the Walkabout Soup of the day, a unique presentation of an Australian favorite.

Hours	Dinner: 4pm – 10:30pm Mon-Thur 4pm – 11:30pm Fri & Sat 4pm – 10pm Sundays
Serving	Dinner
Price	$11 - $24
Reservations	Recommended
Environment	Casual
Cuisine	Beef, Burgers, Chicken, Fish
Outdoor Seating	No
Contact Info.	(206) 262-0326
Notables	❑ Curb-side Take-away

SOUTH LAKE UNION
Yale Street Landing

The Yale Street Landing is a private dock offering transient tie-up for boaters visiting its two restaurants. At the south end of Lake Union, this private dock with its ample tie-up space is an excellent dining destination. There's plenty of space for runabouts and smaller craft with dock ends suitable for one or possibly two larger craft. With some careful piloting, smaller day-cruisers will be able to maneuver in and out of the 12 finger pier slip spaces.

RESTAURANTS
BluWater Bistro
I Love Sushi

The dock is located just a few steps away from the restaurants. To find the Yale Street Landing, look for the BluWater Bistro sign on the building. The dock and tie-up area is located to the north and west of the restaurant and just north of the Kayak rental float.

The Yale Street Landing tie-up area is the entire H-shaped dock. There are 6 double slips that make a snug fit for two runabouts each, or one larger vessel. In addition, there are two shallow water tie-ups on the shore side of this dock. The deep-water end of the dock will accommodate one or two larger vessels.

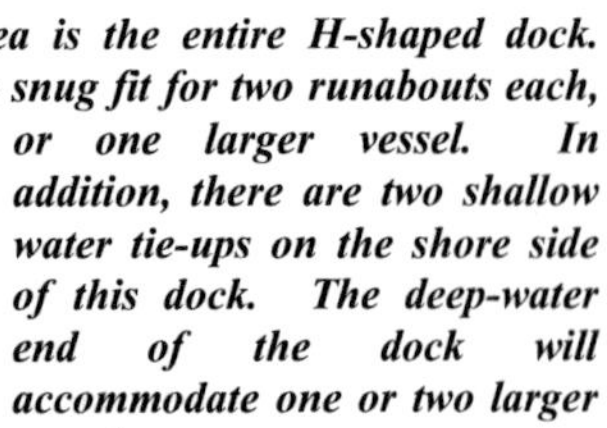

You will find two great restaurants at this location, which are described on the following pages. You will also find The Electric Boat Co., who have started a water taxi service in Lake Union and also rent electric Duffy Cruisers with a 2 hour minimum. For more information call 206-223-7476 and ask for Arnie or Lyssa.

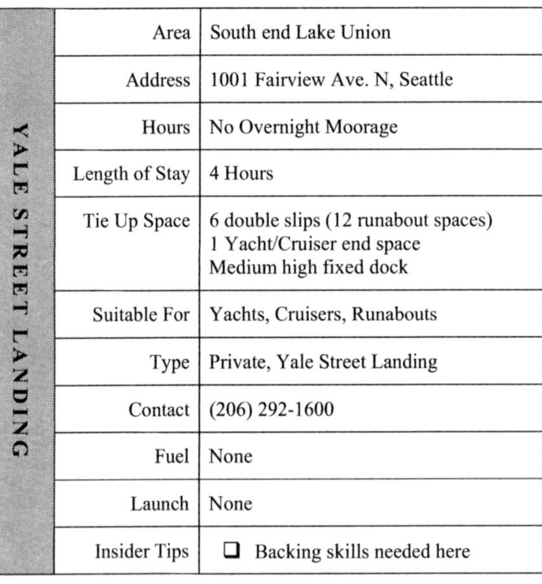

YALE STREET LANDING	
Area	South end Lake Union
Address	1001 Fairview Ave. N, Seattle
Hours	No Overnight Moorage
Length of Stay	4 Hours
Tie Up Space	6 double slips (12 runabout spaces) 1 Yacht/Cruiser end space Medium high fixed dock
Suitable For	Yachts, Cruisers, Runabouts
Type	Private, Yale Street Landing
Contact	(206) 292-1600
Fuel	None
Launch	None
Insider Tips	❑ Backing skills needed here

SOUTH LAKE UNION
Yale Street Landing

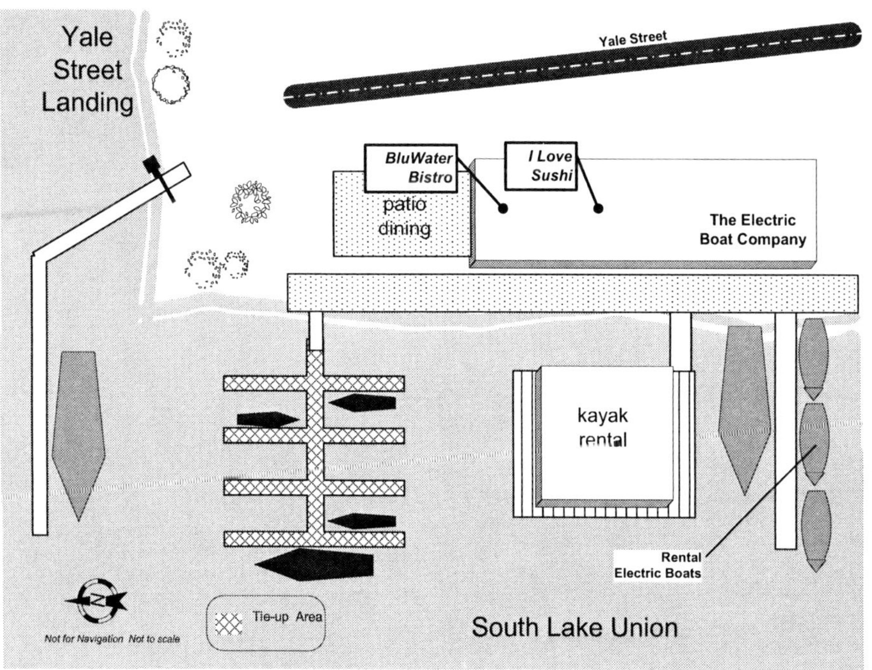

SOUTH LAKE UNION
Yale Street Landing

BLUWATER BISTRO

The true bistro spirit can be found at the BluWater with its small cozy café and lively bar. The heated lakeside patio is very popular in the summer months; and the more formal seating upstairs, provides a nice view over-looking Lake Union and is available Fridays and Saturdays. Since opening in 1997, The BluWater has gained the reputation of being the "in spot," which is most evident after 9 pm. Menu items include fish, pasta, steaks, chicken, burgers, sandwiches, and salads. The BluWater Classic Cobb salad with roasted chicken, avocado, blu cheese, bacon, tomatoes, and vinaigrette is especially good. For lunch try the Portobella Mushroom Sandwich served on a Kaiser roll with provolone and roasted red peppers and basil mayo.

Hours	Lunch: 11:30am - 4pm Daily Dinner: 4pm - 1am Daily
Serving	Lunch, Dinner
Price	$5-$8Lunch $12-$23 Dinner
Reservations	Yes, parties of 8 or more
Environment	Casual / Business Casual
Cuisine	Seafood, Pasta, Chicken, Burgers
Outdoor Seating	Yes, Patio, Summer Months
Contact Info.	(206) 447-0769 www.bluwaterbistro.com
Notables	Popular night spot

I LOVE SUSHI

Sushi lovers swear by I Love Sushi as offering the best sushi in town, the vinegary sweet rice combined with seafood and vegetables both raw and cooked. The white linen tablecloths provide a comfortable setting, while chefs in tall white hats prepare orders. Their Sashimi, strips of raw fish and shellfish, are touted to be the freshest. For the timid, try the shrimp; or the raw tuna with its mild, sweet taste; or the California roll of wrapped rice, avocado, and vegetables. Tempura, fish or vegetables cooked in a fluffy batter, is also available. For the more adventurous, try the Sea eel, salmon, yellowtail, whitefish, squid, and octopus. Presentations of these delicacies are always artful. To complete your sushi experience, try one of the Japanese beers; Asahi, Kirin, or Sapporo. Chilled, premium sake is also available.

Hours	Lunch: 11:30am - 2pm Mon-Fri Dinner: 5pm - 10pm Sun-Thurs 5pm - 10:30pm Fri & Sat
Serving	Lunch, Dinner
Price	$7-$15
Reservations	No (Yes, for 5pm-6:30pm)
Cuisine	Fish, Noodles, Vegetables
Outdoor Seating	No
Contact Info.	(206) 625-9604 www.ilovesushi.com
Notables	❑ Take-Out Available

SOUTH LAKE UNION

Yale Street Landing

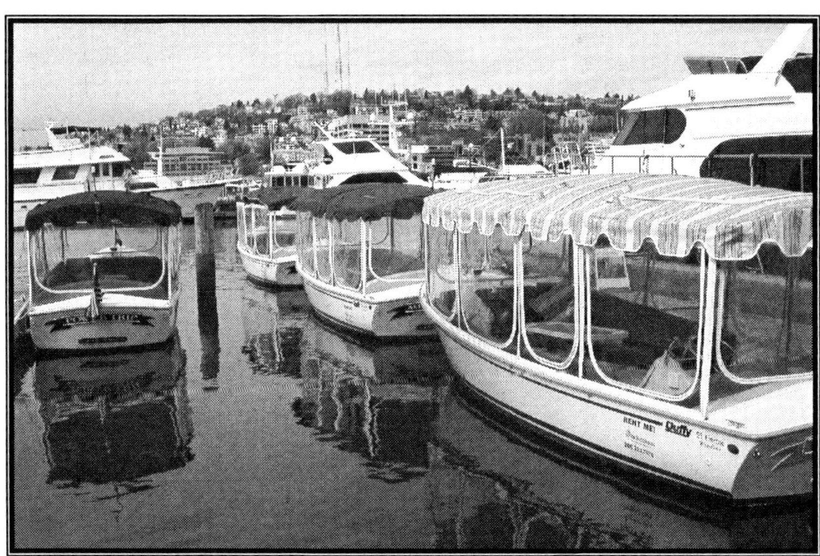

Edmonds Shilshole Bay & Ship Canal

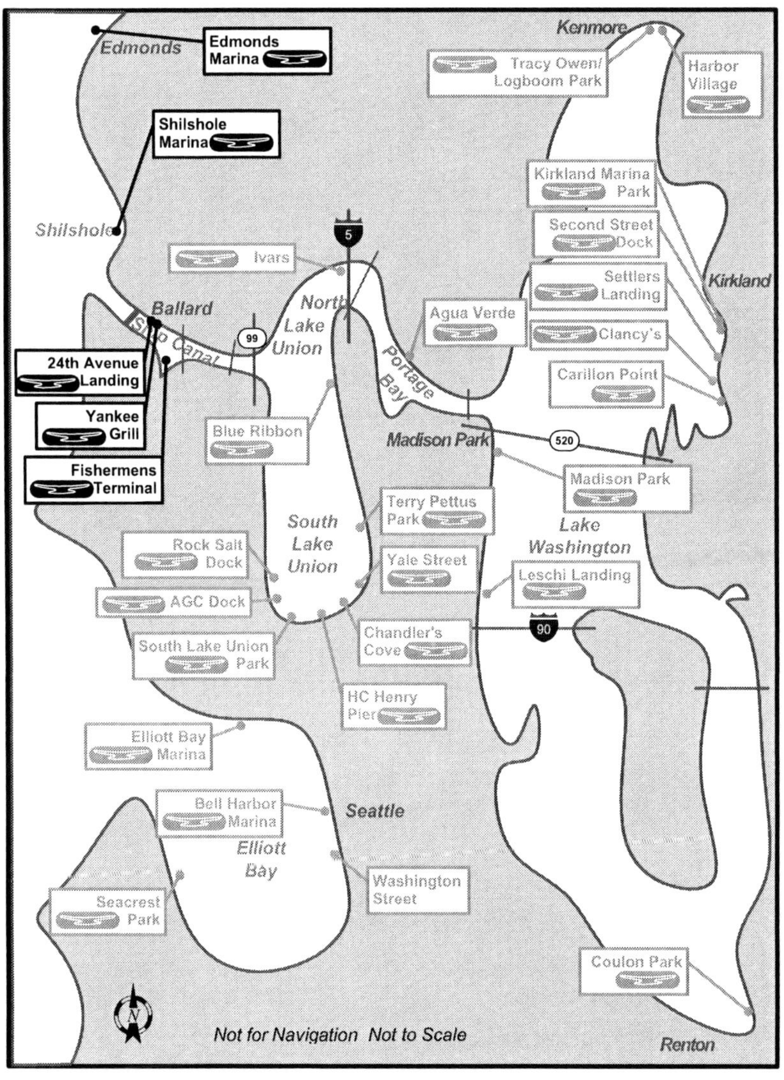

Edmonds
Edmonds Marina
Kenmore
Tracy Owen/ Logboom Park
Harbor Village
Shilshole Marina
Kirkland Marina Park
Shilshole
Second Street Dock
Ivars
5
Settlers Landing
Kirkland
Ballard
North Lake Union
Agua Verde
Ship Canal
99
Clancy's
Portage Bay
24th Avenue Landing
Carillon Point
Yankee Grill
Blue Ribbon
Madison Park
520
Fishermens Terminal
Madison Park
Terry Pettus Park
South Lake Union
Lake Washington
Rock Salt Dock
Yale Street
Leschi Landing
AGC Dock
90
Chandler's Cove
South Lake Union Park
HC Henry Pier
Elliott Bay Marina
Bell Harbor Marina
Seattle
Elliott Bay
Washington Street
Seacrest Park
Coulon Park
Not for Navigation Not to Scale
Renton

EDMONDS

Edmonds Marina

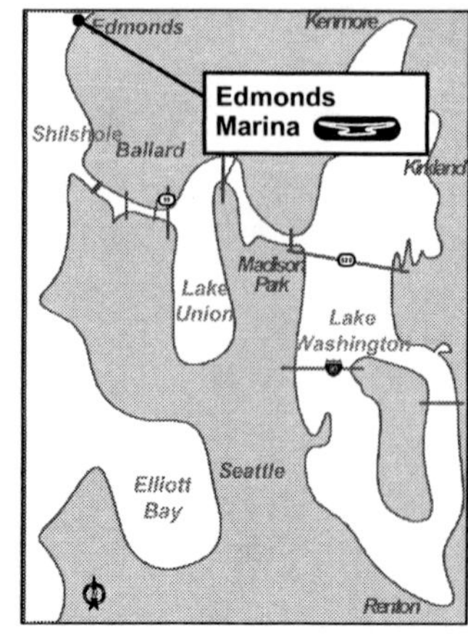

The Port of Edmonds offers Seattle boaters another destination with beautiful views of Puget Sound, sandy beaches, and a lovely seaside promenade. There are four eateries within easy walking distance of the port, which affords beautiful views of Puget Sound and the ferry arrivals and departures from the Edmonds Ferry Dock. The Port of Edmonds guest tie-up space is located on the "I," "J," and "K" docks. The first four hours are free. After four hours, the cost is 70 cents per foot per day. Visiting vessels are required to register upon arrival.

RESTAURANTS
Arnies
Anthony's Beach Café
Anthony's Restaurant

EDMONDS MARINA	
Area	Edmonds
Address	Admiral Way
Hours	All Hours
Length of Stay	4 Hours (no charge) Over 4 Hrs (60¢ per foot)
Tie Up Space	410 Feet
Suitable For	Yachts, Cruisers, Runabouts
Type	Public, Port of Edmonds
Contact	(425) 774-0549 Port Office (425) 775-4588 Harbor Master
Fuel	Yes
Launch	Yes

EDMONDS
Edmonds Marina

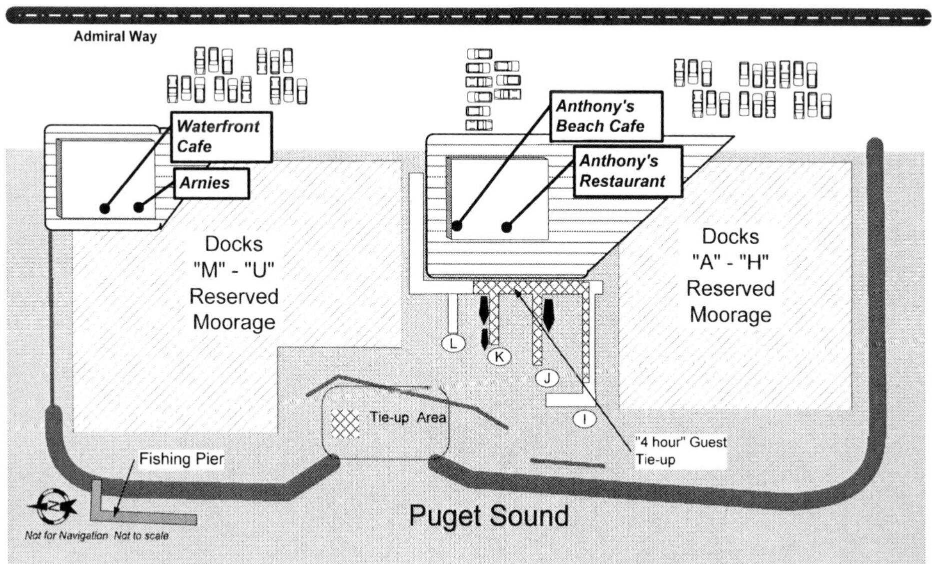

Edmonds Marina
Admiral Way
Waterfront Cafe
Arnies
Anthony's Beach Cafe
Anthony's Restaurant
Docks "M" - "U" Reserved Moorage
Docks "A" - "H" Reserved Moorage
L
K
J
I
Tie-up Area
"4 hour" Guest Tie-up
Fishing Pier
Puget Sound
Not for Navigation Not to scale

EDMONDS
Edmonds Marina

ARNIES

Arnies has been an Edmonds icon for 22 years with spectacular views of the Edmonds waterfront and close-up views of the ferry traffic. The restaurant has an open-floor plan with a large comfortable bar and a covered deck for outdoor dining during the summer months. Arnies serves large salads and sandwiches, along with pasta, seafood favorites, steaks, and chicken. Try the seared fish tacos with citrus marinated mahi mahi fillets seared and wrapped in warm flour tortillas with chipotle-lime mayonnaise, shredded cabbage, and fresh salsa. The pit roasted smoked salmon with lemon beurre blanc and fried capers is also good. Arnies offers an early bird three-course dinner for $16 from 4 pm to 6 pm, Sunday through Thursday.

Hours	Brunch: 10am – 2pm Sundays Lunch: 11:30am – 4pm Mon-Sat Dinner: 4pm – 9pm Sun-Thur 4pm – 10pm Fri & Sat Happy Hour: 3pm – 6pm Mon-Fri
Serving	Brunch, Lunch, Dinner
Price	$10-$17 Brunch $9-$15 Lunch/Dinner
Reservations	Recommended
Environment	Business Casual / Dressy
Cuisine	Seafood, Chicken, Pasta
Outdoor Seating	Yes, Deck, Summer Months
Contact Info.	(425) 771-5688

ANTHONY'S BEACH CAFE

This fun café with its beach theme has colorful ribbon-fish hanging from the ceilings and check out the swimming suits on the human wood figures on the his and hers bathroom doors. Planter boxes just outside the windows are filled with beautiful tulips of different colors and there is even a sandbox with toys for the children. The Beach Café offers "beach salads," "beach tacos," "beach bowls and baskets," burgers, grilled chicken, and seafood. A house favorite is the Hawaiian Cobb Salad with fresh mango, bacon, avocado, tomato, won tons & baby shrimp on seasonal market greens with basil vinaigrette & crumbled blue cheese. Another favorite is the Barbequed Garlic Prawns with garlic butter, Cajun spices, basil, and red potatoes.

Hours	Lunch/Dinner: 11am – 9pm Mon-Thur 11am – 9:45pm Fri & Sat Noon – 9pm Sundays
Serving	Lunch, Dinner
Price	$6-$15 Lunch/Dinner
Reservations	Recommended
Environment	Casual
Cuisine	Seafood, Burgers, Salads
Outdoor Seating	Yes, Patio, Summer Months
Contact Info.	(425) 771-4400

EDMONDS
Edmonds Marina

ANTHONY'S RESTAURANT

There are numerous Anthony restaurants in the greater Seattle area and this is yet another Anthony's not to be missed with great views of Puget Sound and grand evening sunsets. A separate modern bar is available for fine wines and brews along with a dining area with large corner windows to capture the view of the Sound and ferry traffic. The main area of the restaurant has a combination of tables and booths along the length of the restaurant, all with the same grand views. An outdoor open deck is available for seating during the summer months. As at all Anthony restaurants, fresh seafood is offered along with steaks and pasta dishes. Dungeness Crab is always a favorite at Anthony's in addition to oysters, scallops, and lobster.

Hours	Dinner: 4:30pm – 9:30pm Mon-Thur 4:30pm – 10pm Fri & Sat 3:30pm – 9pm Sundays
Serving	Dinner
Price	$17-$30
Reservations	Recommended
Environment	Business Casual / Dressy
Cuisine	Seafood, Steaks
Outdoor Seating	Yes, Deck, Summer Months
Contact Info.	(425) 771-4400 www.anthonys.com

WATERFRONT CAFE

The Waterfront Café is located downstairs from Arnies Restaurant and serves breakfast and lunch items. Enjoy a cup of homemade chili or chowder along with a crisp salad for lunch or a basket of fish 'n chips or chicken strips. Sandwiches, hot dogs, and hamburgers are also available. This small café has a surprisingly large breakfast menu, including bacon, sausage, hotcakes, eggs, omelets, French Toast, and sticky buns, among other traditional breakfast items.

Hours	Breakfast/Lunch/Dinner: 7am – 7pm Daily Winter Hours Vary
Serving	Breakfast, Lunch, Dinner
Price	$4-$10
Reservations	No
Environment	Casual
Cuisine	Eggs, Fish, Burgers
Outdoor Seating	No
Contact Info.	(425) 743-9590 Ask for the Cafe

SHILSHOLE BAY
Shilshole Marina

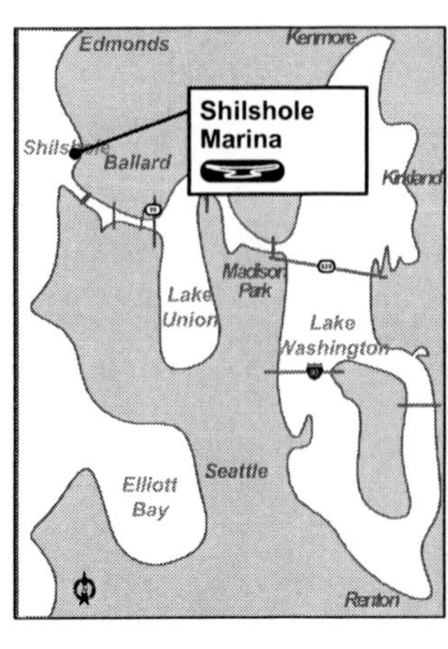

Shilshole Bay Marina is the largest marina in the Seattle area with 1,500 boat slips. The Port of Seattle is currently upgrading the facility and replacing 22 docks and piers as well as replacing and expanding the sailing center at the north end of the Marina. Docks and boats will be shifted around while construction is underway. Visitors need to register and pay at the Marina Office. Self-registration booths are located both inside and outside the Office. Short term stays of 0-6 hours at 25 cents per foot are available until the end of May 2006, after which guest space will be removed until construction is completed in 2007 or 2008. Call the Marina for the latest status and as availability continues to change.

RESTAURANTS
Anthony's Home Port
Little Coney
The Purple Cow
Ray's Boathouse

New service buildings, a new office administration building, restrooms, showers, storage, and laundry are included in the project. A pad will be provided for the private development of a new Anthony's restaurant with guest moorage for visiting boaters. Charlie's Bar & Grill, which was previously located inside the marina office administration building is now closed.

Ray's Boathouse & Café, The Purple Cow, Little Coney, and Anthony's Homeport restaurant on Seaview Avenue West, are all within walking distance of Shilshole Bay Marina.

SHILSHOLE MARINA	
Area	Shilshole Bay
Address	7001 Seaview Ave NW Seattle
Hours	All Hours
Length of Stay	6 Hours Additional Overnight Rates Closed after May 2006
Tie Up Space	100 + Guest Moorage Spaces Limited Space During Construction
Suitable For	Yachts, Cruiser, Runabouts
Type	Public, Port of Seattle
Contact	(206) 601-4089 or (206) 728-3006 Channel 17 on your VHF
Fuel	Yes
Launch	North of Marina (Eddie Vine Boat Ramp)
Insider Tips	❑ Marina Currently Under Renovation ❑ No Guest Space after May 27, 2006

SHILSHOLE BAY
Shilshole Marina

North Central Pier
Guest Moorage
Rafting Permitted up to 3 boats deep.

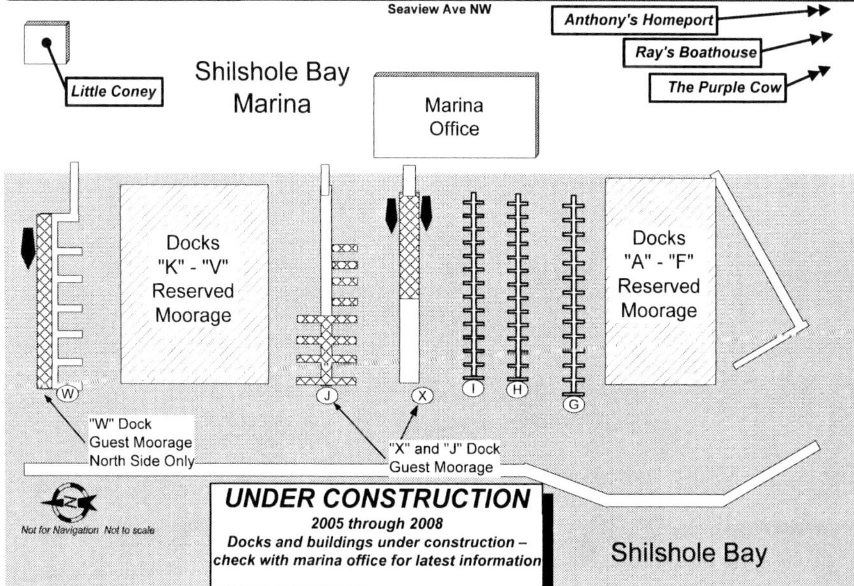
Seaview Ave NW
Anthony's Homeport
Ray's Boathouse
The Purple Cow
Little Coney
Shilshole Bay Marina
Marina Office
Docks "K" - "V" Reserved Moorage
Docks "A" - "F" Reserved Moorage
W
J
X
I
H
G
"W" Dock Guest Moorage North Side Only
"X" and "J" Dock Guest Moorage
N
Not for Navigation Not to scale
UNDER CONSTRUCTION
2005 through 2008
Docks and buildings under construction – check with marina office for latest information
Shilshole Bay

SHILSHOLE BAY
Shilshole Marina

ANTHONY'S HOMEPORT SHILSHOLE

Walk south from Shilshole Bay Marina for approximately one-quarter mile to reach Anthony's at 6135 Seaview Ave. West. This unique location puts you in a seafarer's mood as you gaze out at the expanse of Puget Sound, the shipping lanes, and the Olympic Mountains. Anthony's completes the relaxing atmosphere with wooden chairs, fish motif carpets, and a large fish tank room divider. Here you will find fresh seafood dishes such as the Yellowfin Ahi, the Alder planked Salmon, or the oven roasted Halibut. Anthony's fresh seafood comes from their seafood company, which was started in 1985 and is located on Pier 91 in Seattle. The full service bar has ample out-door summer seating to enjoy the sea breezes.

Hours	Brunch: 10am-2pm Sundays Dinner: 4:30pm-9:30pm Mon-Thu 4:30pm-10pm Fri-Sat 3:30pm-9:30pm Sundays
Serving	Brunch, Dinner
Price	\$9-\$17 Brunch \$16-\$30 Dinner
Reservations	Recommended
Environment	Business Casual
Cuisine	Seafood, Steak
Outdoor Seating	Yes, Deck/Patio, Summer Months
Contact Info.	(206) 783-0780 www.anthonys.com
Notables	❑ Sunday Crab Feed (all you can eat)

SHILSHOLE BAY
Shilshole Marina

LITTLE CONEY

Little Coney, located at 8003 Seaview Ave. NW, is on the north end of Shilshole Bay Marina next to the Eddie Vine Boat Ramp. This cute little stucco building has several outdoor picnic tables where you can view Puget Sound and the boat ramp activity. Little Coney fits the beach theme of fish 'n chips, burgers, hotdogs, drinks, sandwiches, and ice cream. The Golden Gardens Park is just on the north side of the boat ramp and has beautiful sandy beaches and expansive views of Puget Sound. Renovation of the old 1929 Bathhouse at the Park has recently been completed by the City of Seattle and is open during the summers. Little Coney is conveniently located next to the Park.

Hours	Summers: 9am - 9pm Daily Winter/Spring: 10am - 6pm Daily
Serving	Lunch, Dinner
Price	$2-$10
Reservations	No
Environment	Casual
Cuisine	Fish and Chips, Burgers, Hotdogs
Outdoor Seating	Yes, Patio, Summer Months
Contact Info.	(206) 782-6598

THE PURPLE COW

The Purple Cow is located about one-quarter mile south of Shilshole Bay Marina at 6301 Seaview NW, between Anthony's and the West Marine supply store. You can't miss the eye-catching purple cow on top of the building, or the inviting deck enclosed with a painted wood lattice. The Purple Cow serves soups and freshly made sandwiches. Fruit-filled scones are their signature item along with other baked goodies, including bagels, muffins, coffee cakes, cookies, and brownies. Espresso and organic coffee is available along with delicious smoothies like the popular "Purple Cow," which is made from blueberries, cranberries, and strawberries.

Hours	6:30am - 5pm Mon-Fri 7:30am - 4pm Saturdays 8am – 3pm Sundays
Serving	Breakfast, Lunch
Price	$2-$10
Reservations	No
Environment	Casual
Cuisine	Baked goods, Soups, Sandwiches,
Outdoor Seating	Yes, Deck, Summer Months
Contact Info.	(206) 784-1417

SHILSHOLE BAY
Shilshole Marina

RAY'S BOATHOUSE & CAFE

Ray's is located one-quarter mile south of Shilshole Bay Marina at 6049 Seaview Ave. NW. Ray's Boathouse & Café is named after Ray Lichtenberger, who located his boat rental and bait house on this site in 1939, and in 1945 added a coffee house. Ray's has long been a Seattle icon and boaters are very familiar with Ray's 1952 red neon sign seen west of the Locks. Beautiful views of Puget Sound and the Olympic Mountains can be enjoyed from both the Boathouse dining room downstairs, and the more casual Café with its outdoor deck upstairs. Ray's has received rave reviews in Gourmet Magazine and Food & Wine. Award-winning wines are available in more than 400 varieties. The Café offers 20 microbrews and hard-to-get classic European-style beers. Boathouse classic menu items include wood smoked Black Cod, Prawns split and baked in hazelnut-coriander butter, and grilled Alaskan Halibut with herb potatoes and Savoy cabbage to name just a few. The upstairs Café offers dishes like Red Rockfish served with polenta, grilled Salmon burger, and crab and shrimp cakes.

Hours	Boathouse: 5pm - 9pm Sun-Thur 5pm - 10pm Fri & Sat Café: 11:30am - 10pm Sun & Sat Happy Hour: 4pm - 6pm And 10pm - 12am Daily
Serving	Lunch, Dinner
Price	$22-$45 Boathouse $13-$17 Cafe
Reservations	Recommended
Environment	Casual / Business Casual
Cuisine	Seafood, Pastas, Salads, Burgers, Lamb, Chicken, Steak
Outdoor Seating	Yes, Café Deck, Summer Months
Contact Info.	(206) 789-3770 Boathouse (206) 782-0094 Café (206) 789-6309 Catering www.rays.com
Notables	❑ Ray's Boathouse Seafood Secrets cookbook ❑ Annual Springtime Celebration ❑ On-line Reservations

SHILSHOLE BAY
Shilshole Marina

Dress warmly for the
evening ride home.

SHIP CANAL
Fishermen's Terminal

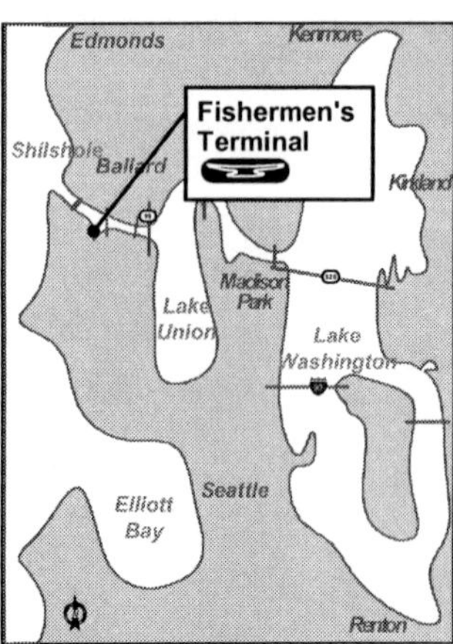

Fishermen's Terminal has been the home of the Pacific Northwest fishing fleet since 1913 with over 700 commercial fishing vessels. This historic location has a beautiful memorial in honor of those lost at sea as well as several interesting historical markers. Guest moorage is available for up to 2 hours while visiting Fishermen's Terminal. In addition to a fine dining experience, you will enjoy boating past a wide variety of fishing vessels ranging from 30-foot gill-netters to 300-foot factory trawlers.

RESTAURANTS
Caffe Appassionato
Chinook's
Little Chinook's
Bay Cafe
Highliner Pub

To find the guest moorage at Fishermen's Terminal, go south along the west side of the Ballard Bridge until you see the Fishermen's Terminal sign to the southwest, then turn west and follow the channel. Next to the last pier/channel, turn south. At the end of the channel you will see signs for guest moorage.

This interesting location has an excellent coffee shop and four eateries from which to choose and you can also buy groceries at the Fishermen's Grocery Food Market. If you are looking for fresh fish to take home to cook or freeze, don't miss the Wild Salmon Seafood Market located on the south side of Chinooks Restaurant.

Visitors can also buy portioned fresh and frozen fish directly from local fishermen at Fishermen's Terminal. Off-the-boat sales occur along the West Wall, a seawall that forms the western boundary of the boat basin at the Terminal. Hours for fish sales vary, for an update, call (206) 728-3301.

Don't miss the Fishermen's Fall Festival, which is held in September on the boardwalk of the Terminal with fun fishing theme activities for children and adults. Proceeds from the activities within the festival are donated to the Seattle Fishermen's Memorial Foundation.

FISHERMEN'S TERMINAL	
Area	South side of Ship Canal, Fishermen's Terminal, Salmon Bay, West of Ballard Bridge
Address	1900 W. Nickerson St., Seattle
Hours	All Hours
Length of Stay	2 hours
Tie Up Space	125 foot floating dock
Suitable For	Cruiser, Runabouts
Type	Public, Port of Seattle
Contact	(206) 728-3112
Fuel	None
Launch	None
Insider Tips	❑ In the Plaza, stop and read the commemorative and historical plaques ❑ Fishermen's Fall Festival – Sept

SHIP CANAL
Fishermen's Terminal

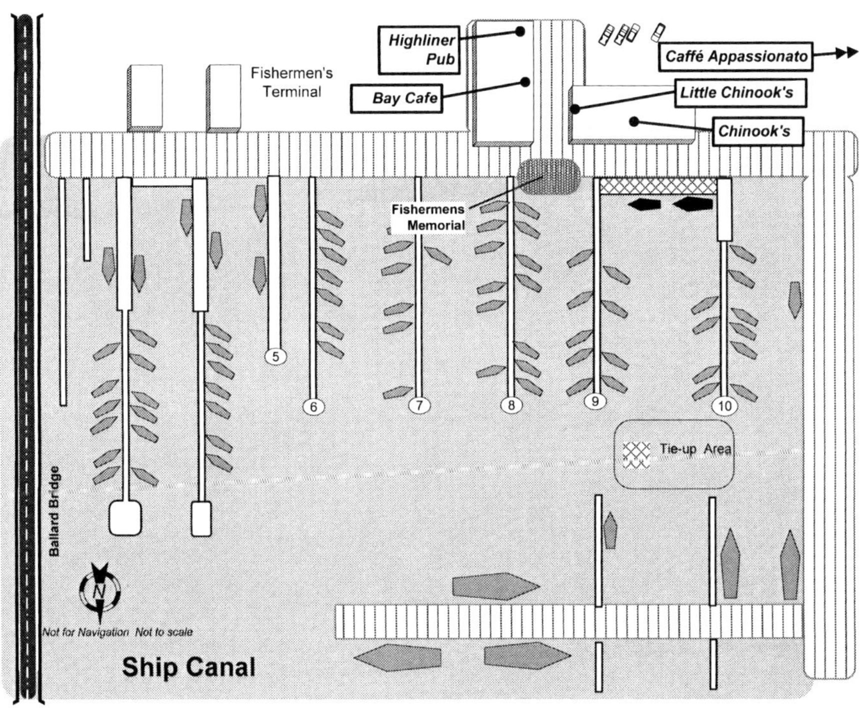

SHIP CANAL
Fishermen's Terminal

CHINOOKS

Chinook's at Salmon Bay is a casual, high-energy seafood restaurant located at Fishermen's Terminal. Salmon, Halibut, and Crab is the essence of Chinook's. Other fresh seafood entrees include Trout, scampi, and oysters. Although the specialty is fresh Northwest seafood, Chinook's extensive menu offers beef, chicken, and vegetarian fare. This great family restaurant sports a cannery motif and is popular with local fishermen and tourists alike. Chinook's also has a very nice breakfast menu. The large windows provide a great view of Salmon Bay and the Pacific Northwest fishing fleet. Chinooks is home for the Husky Party Boat taking football game attendees to the University of Washington Husky Stadium. For more information, call 206-283-Hook.

Hours	Breakfast: 7:30am - 11:30pm Sat & Sun Lunch: 11am - 4pm Mon-Fri 11:30am - 4pm Saturdays Dinner: 4pm - 10pm Mon-Thur 4pm – 11pm Fri & Sat 1:30pm - 10pm Sundays
Serving	Breakfast, Lunch, Dinner
Price	$7-$10 Breakfast $7-$15 Lunch $7-$20 Dinner
Reservations	Parties of 15 or more
Environment	Casual
Cuisine	Seafood
Outdoor Seating	Yes, End-Patio, Summer Months
Contact Info.	(206) 283-4665 www.anthonys.com
Notables	❑ Home of the Chinook's Husky Dawg Party Boat

LITTLE CHINOOKS

Little Chinook's is a classic Seattle waterfront quick seafood service restaurant offering fish 'n chips and to-go orders. This seafood bar has an indoor seating area for inclement weather. Outdoor seating is available in the plaza overlooking the fishing boats. Be sure to check out the commemorative and historical plaques in the plaza.

Hours	Lunch/Dinner: 11am - 8pm Daily
Serving	Lunch, Dinner
Price	$5-$8
Reservations	No
Cuisine	Fast Food Seafood and Chowder
Outdoor Seating	Yes, Patio, Summer Months
Contact Info.	(206) 283-4665
Notables	❑ Espresso Bar ❑ To-Go orders

SHIP CANAL
Fishermen's Terminal

BAY CAFE

The Bay Café at Fishermen's Terminal is like stepping back in time with its 50's motif serving American favorites. They still make their soups and mashed potatoes from scratch and still provide that old- fashioned service without the computers. The chef's daily specials, like halibut, snapper, and oysters, can be found on the menu board. Breakfast includes omelets, ham & eggs, and French toast. "Eggs Benedict" is served on weekends. People from all walks of life still come to the Bay Café to enjoy the atmosphere and a window view of Seattle's Fishing Fleet.

Hours	Breakfast: 6:30am - 2:15pm Mon-Fri 7am - 2:15pm Sat & Sun Lunch: 10:30am - 2:15pm Daily
Serving	Breakfast, Lunch
Price	$8-$12
Reservations	Accepted for parties of 8 or more
Environment	Casual
Cuisine	Fish, American Favorites
Environment	Casual
Outdoor Seating	No
Contact Info.	(206) 282-3435

HIGHLINER PUB

The Highliner Pub is located on the southeast corner of the Fishermen's Terminal Plaza. The Pub serves burgers, fish 'n chips, salads, chicken strips, sandwiches, and homemade soups, including clam chowder. This rustic fishermen's pub has electronic darts, a pool table, and a large screen television. Live blues music and/or live folk music is held on Friday and Saturday nights from 9 pm to 10 pm.

Hours	11am - 11pm Mon-Thur 11am – 1am Fri & Sat 11am – close Sundays Hours Vary
Serving	Lunch, Dinner
Price	$5-$12
Reservations	No
Environment	Pub Casual
Cuisine	Burgers, Fish 'n Chips, Salads, Sandwiches
Environment	Casual
Outdoor Seating	Yes, Patio, Summer Months
Contact Info.	(206) 283-2233

SHIP CANAL

Fishermen's Terminal

CAFFE APPASSIONATO

The Caffe Appassionato is a tucked away gem near Fishermen's Terminal. To locate the Caffe, walk west from Chinooks through the west parking lot; you will find a worn path through the shrubs where folks pass to cross 21st Avenue W. to the corner of West Emerson Place. You will find fresh, good tasting lattes and espressos here as the Caffe Appassionato roasts their own coffee beans in-house, where you can watch the roasting process. The attractive building has a lovely arbor entrance with outdoor seating and the interior has beautiful mahogany wood pillars and sectional arched ceiling work. This interesting building served as a boat engine house in earlier times. The Caffe Appassionato has perfected their slow roasting process to produce full-bodied, aromatic coffee that is less acidic and gentle on the stomach. So go ahead and enjoy that cup of coffee along with their selection of cookies and pastries.

Hours	6am – 6pm Mon-Fri 6am – 4pm Sat & Sun
Serving	Espresso
Price	$3 - $5
Reservations	N/A
Environment	Casual
Cuisine	Espresso, Cookies, Pastries
Outdoor Seating	Yes, Patio, Summer Months
Contact Info.	(206) 281-8040
Notables	❑ In-house Roasting ❑ Order beans for delivery

Fishermen's Terminal

SHIP CANAL
Yankee Grill Guest Dock

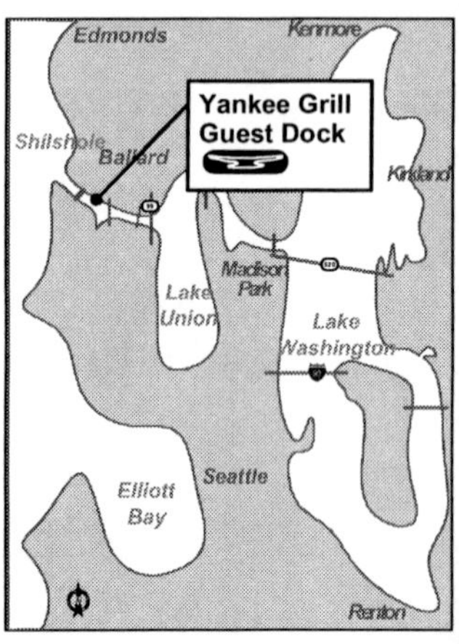

The Yankee Grill is located at the north side of the Ship Canal just east of the Chittenden Locks. Boating guests dining at The Yankee Grill can either tie-up at The Yankee Grill's private dock or at the public dock located next door to the restaurant.

The Yankee Grill's private dock is located on the west corner of the restaurant building and has room for one or two boats. If the Yankee Grill's moorage is full, there will most likely be space available at the public dock (see 24th Avenue Landing), which is located immediately west of The Yankee Grill. It is just a short walk from the public dock to The Yankee Grill.

RESTAURANT	
	Yankee Grill

YANKEE GRILL GUEST DOCK		
	Area	West end of Ship Canal just east of the Chittenden Locks
	Address	5300 24th Avenue NW, Seattle
	Length of Stay	While Dining
	Tie Up Space	60 feet of tie-up space
	Suitable For	Yachts, Cruisers, Runabouts
	Type	Private, Yankee Grill
	Contact	(206) 783-1964
	Fuel	Ballard Oil to the west
	Launch	None
	Insider Tips	❑ CAUTION – watch for the large rocks/concrete at the shallow end of tie-up area.

CLOSED

SHIP CANAL
Yankee Grill Guest Dock

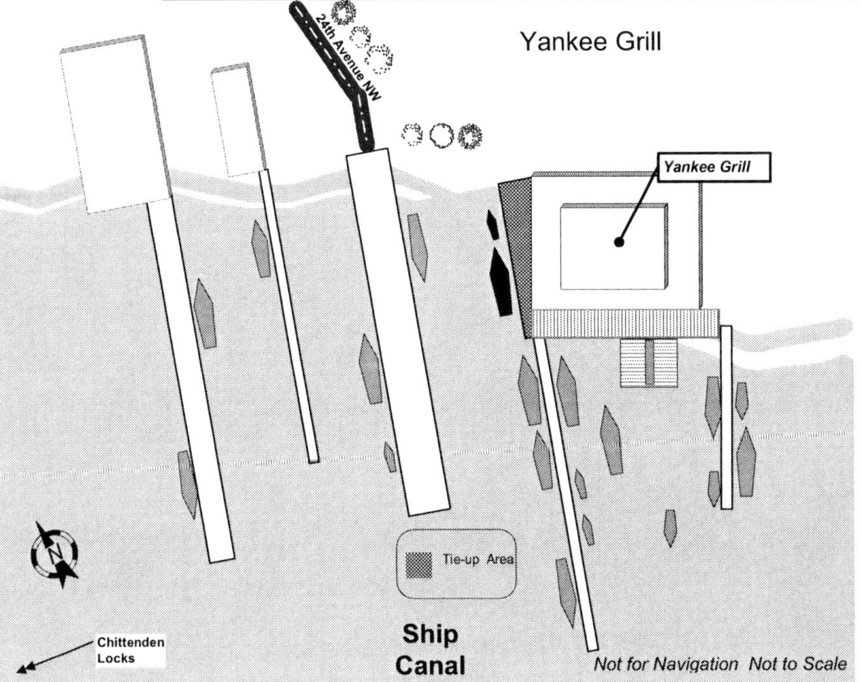

SHIP CANAL
Yankee Grill Guest Dock

CLOSED

YANKEE GRILL

This comfortable restaurant provides views of the ship canal from 90 percent of its seating and serves home-style cooked meals. Specialties include rotisserie turkey, rotisserie chicken, prime rib, pot roast, and meatloaf. Other selections include seafood, pastas, burgers, steaks, and sandwiches. Dinner portions are quite large, which makes this venue a favorite family restaurant. Breakfast is very popular at the Yankee Grill; and there is rarely a wait due to the spacious restaurant seating. Breakfast items include omelets, crepes, waffles, eggs, hashbrowns, and several Eggs Benedict specialties. During the summers you can sit out on the deck, which overlooks the ship canal. The Yankee Grill is a great family stop before or after a day of boating and is conveniently located on the fresh-water side of the Locks.

Hours	Breakfast: 8am - 11am Daily Lunch: 11am - 4pm Daily Dinner: 4pm - 10pm Mon-Sat 4pm – 9pm Sundays
Serving	Breakfast, Lunch, Dinner
Price	$5-12
Reservations	Yes, Party of 8 or more
Environment	Casual
Cuisine	Roast, Turkey, Prime Rib, Seafood
Outdoor Seating	Yes, Deck, Summer Months
Contact Info.	(206) 783-1964

Yankee Grill Guest Dock

SHIP CANAL
24th Avenue Landing

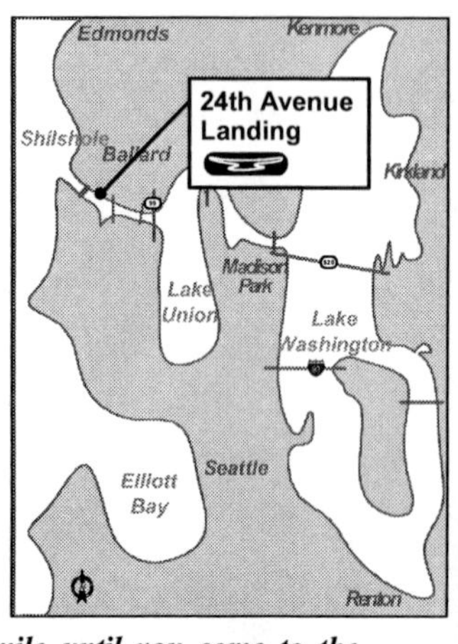

Ballard's 24th Avenue Landing is a community constructed and maintained public dock offering boaters access to their community. Boats of 40 feet or less are welcome to tie-up and visit the area restaurants, shops, markets, and entertainment located within easy walking distance. No overnight moorage is permitted.

RESTAURANTS	
	Coffee & Tea (9)
	Casual Dining (18)
	Fine Dining (4)
	Fast Food (8)

In addition to enjoying the many dining establishments of Ballard, you can view the locks, which allow boats to pass to and from the fresh water lakes and the salt water of Puget Sound. Walk west on Market Street for approximately one half mile until you come to the Hiram Chittenden Locks and Park.

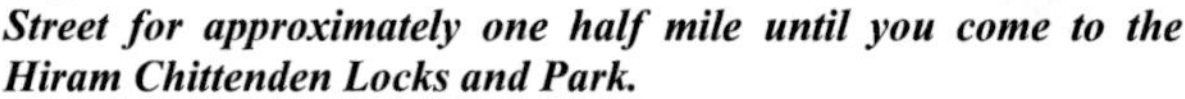

To find "Old Ballard," walk east along NW Market Street and then turn right heading south on Ballard Ave. NW. Many of the brick and wood buildings date back to the late 1800's. This Scandinavian community was named after Captain William Ballard, who planned and incorporated it in 1888 and in 1906 was annexed by Seattle.

Special events in Ballard include a Scandinavian parade in May and Seafood Fest in July. A Farmer's Market is held every Sunday from 10 am to 4 pm starting May 5th through November 3rd at NW 56th Street and 22nd Avenue NW.

24TH AVENUE LANDING		
	Area	North Side of West End of Ship Canal
	Address	5300 24th Avenue NW, Seattle
	Hours	No Overnight Moorage
	Length of Stay	9 Hours
	Tie Up Space	300 feet of high fixed dock
	Suitable For	Yachts, Cruisers, Runabouts
	Type	Public, Ballard Community
	Contact	(206) 684-4060
	Fuel	Ballard Oil (Mobil) just to the west
	Launch	None
	Insider Tips	❑ 40 foot maximum boat length

SHIP CANAL

24th Avenue Landing

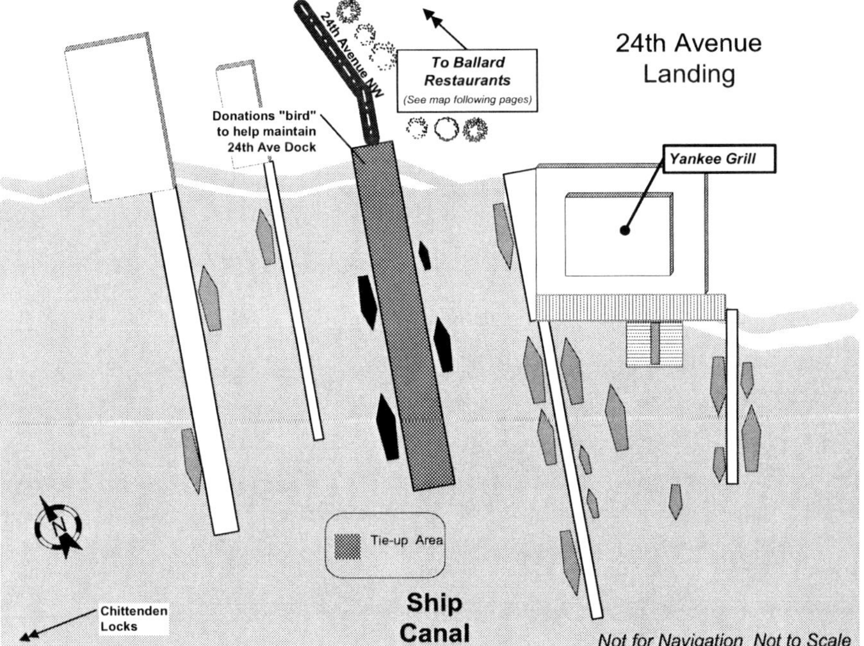

SHIP CANAL
24th Avenue Landing

COFFEE & DESSERTS			
Ben & Jerry's	Ice Cream, Yogurt, Smoothies, Coffee	2038 NW Market St.	(206) 784-4454
Café Besalu	Espresso, Pastries	5909 24th Ave. NW	(206) 789-1463
Chai House	Tea, Bagels, Sandwiches	5463 Leary Ave. NW	(206) 297-2424
Cugini Café	Coffee, Tea	5306 Ballard Ave. NW	(206) 784-2576
Floating Leaves Tea	Tea, Classes	2213 NW Market St.	(206) 529-4268
Java Bean	Espresso, Pastries	5819 – 24th Ave. NW	(206) 788-9677
Nervous Nellie's	Espresso, Pastries	2315 NW Market St.	(206) 706-1095
Starbucks Coffee	Coffee, Pastries	2204 NW Market St.	(206) 782-2795
Tully's Coffee	Coffee, Pastries	2060 NW Market St.	(206) 781-4887

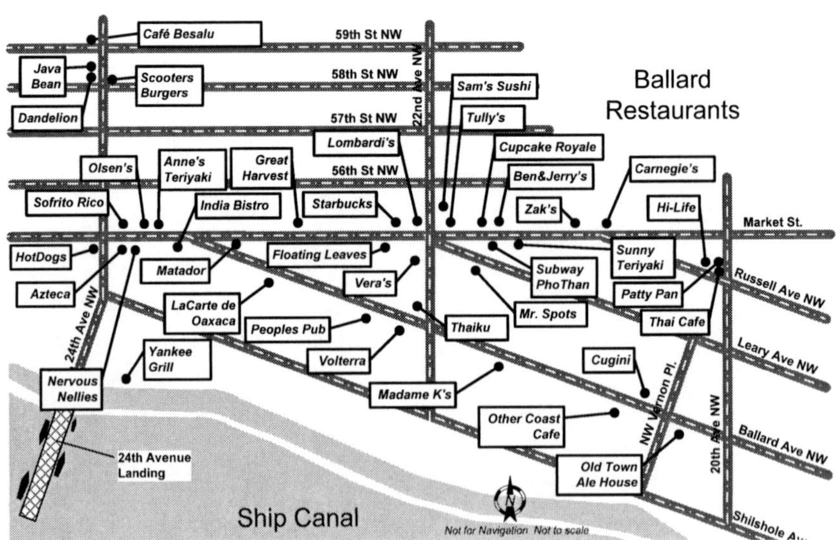

SHIP CANAL
24th Avenue Landing

FINE DINING RESTAURANTS			
Carnegie's	Duck, Lamb, Seafood	2026 NW Market St.	(206) 789-6643
India Bistro	Chicken, Lamb, Veg.	2301 NW Market St.	(206) 783-5080
Thaiku	Noodles, Chicken	5410 Ballard Ave. NW	(206) 706-7807
Volterra	Italian Cuisine	5411 Ballard Ave. NW	(206) 789-5100

CASUAL DINING RESTAURANTS			
Anne's Teriyaki	Chicken, Pork, Noodles	2246 NW Market St.	(206) 789-5838
Azteca Mexican	Mexican Cuisine	2319 NW Market St.	(206) 782-7079
Dandelion	Seafood, Chicken, Steaks, Pasta	5809 – 24th Ave. NW	(206) 817-2416
Hi-Life	Breakfast, Pizza, Sandwiches, Soups	5425 Russell Ave. NW	(206) 784-7272
LaCarte de Oaxaca	Mexican Dishes	5431 Ballard Ave. NW	(206) 782-8722
Lombardi's Cucina	Pizza, Pasta, Veal	2200 NW Market St.	(206) 783-0055
Madame K's Pizza	Pizza, Pasta	5327 Ballard Ave. NW	(206) 783-9710
Matador, The	Burgers, Sandwiches	2221 NW Market St.	(206) 297-2855
Old Town Ale House	Pastas, Sandwiches	5233 Ballard Ave. NW	(206) 782-8323
Other Coast Cafe	Sandwiches	5315 Ballard Ave. NW	(206) 789-0936
Patty Pan Grill	Mexican Cuisine	5402 – 20th Ave. NW	(206) 782-1558
People's Pub	German Food Dishes	5429 Ballard Ave. NW	(206) 783-6521
Pho Than Brothers	Tai Cuisine	2021 NW Market St.	(206) 782-5715
Sam's Sushi Bar/Grill	Sushi, Sashimi, Tofu	5506 22nd Ave. NW	(206) 783-2262
Scooter's Burgers	Burgers, Sandwiches	5802 – 24th Ave. NW	(206) 782-2966
Sofrito Rico	Puerto Rican	2320 NW Market St.	(206) 789-0516
Thai Café	Thai Cuisine	5401 – 20th Ave. NW	(206) 784-4599
Vera's	Omelets, Sandwiches	5417 – 22nd Ave. NW	(206) 782-9966

SHIP CANAL
24th Avenue Landing

FAST FOOD RESTAURANTS			
Cupcake Royale & Verite Coffee	Cupcakes, Coffee, Sandwiches	2052 NW Market St.	(206) 782-9557
Great Harvest Bread	Soup & Sandwiches	2218 NW Market St.	(206) 706-3434
Matt's Gourmet Hot Dogs	Hot Dogs, Sausages, Sandwiches	Market and 24th	(206) 789-1144
Olsen's Scandinavian Food Store	Scandinavian Store Food Items	2248 NW Market St.	(206) 783-8288
Subway	Sandwiches & Salads	2021 NW Market St.	(206) 297-2080
Sunny Teriyaki	Yakisoba, Gyoza	2035 NW Market St.	(206) 781-7839
The Tall Grass Bakery	Fresh Baked Breads	5907 – 24th Ave. NW	(206) 706-0991
Zak's	Burgers, Salads	2040 NW Market St.	(206) 706-ZAKS

Notes